EXMOOR
BY THE WAY

Hilary Binding

HALSGROVE

First published in Great Britain in 2009

British Library Cataloguing-in-Publication Data
A CIP record for this title is available from the British Library

ISBN 978 1 84114 950 9

HALSGROVE
Halsgrove House,
Ryelands Industrial Estate,
Bagley Road, Wellington, Somerset TA21 9PZ
Tel: 01823 653777   Fax: 01823 216796
email: sales@halsgrove.com

Part of the Halsgrove group of companies
Information on all Halsgrove titles is available at: www.halsgrove.com

Printed and bound by Short Run Press, Exeter

CONTENTS

PREFACE

The *West Somerset Free Press* was founded in 1860 by Samuel Cox of Williton. Twelve years later a column, *Notes of the Week*, a commentary on recent local events, began to appear intermittently. On 30 April 1881 Proteus, almost certainly Clement Kille, wrote the first *Notes by the Way* prefacing it with these words: 'As an outsider looking on, interested in the various events passing around, but more especially in this neighbourhood, I purpose making a few notes and remarks from time to time on the people and things which may happen to come under my notice but in so doing I trust I may never exceed the bounds of fair criticism, nor overstep the limits of good taste by noticing in this column matters which it would have been better to pass by unregarded.'

In 1884 the column was taken on by a mysterious X who moved to West Somerset from the Midlands that year. He seemed to spend most of his week hunting and reading *The Globe* and was always very polite about the MP, Sir Alexander Acland Hood. Then in 1909 X was forced to unmask himself and openly engage in a debate he had started over the need for a school in Roadwater. The following week there was W.H. Farrar, writing a letter to the *West Somerset Free Press* to defend his earlier Note.

Farrar continued to write *Notes by the Way* until 1923. He became ill in the autumn of the previous year and Herbert Kille covered his absences for a few weeks. On 5 January 1923 Farrar writes: 'After five week's silence I once more resume my pen, almost rusty with disuse and with the first week of the new year attempt in my usual column of *NBTW*, a title that is now scarcely applicable since during the winter season I find a cosy fireside much too cheerful to leave of an evening to ramble abroad in search of topic; and as news does not readily flow in through shut doors and closed windows, the columns of the daily paper have to be resorted to for pegs whereon to hand a few remarks. If for a while therefore my *Notes* savour more of the fireside than the "way" I hope my readers will judge them leniently; and in return my column will be more regular in the future than in the past, always provided however that Mr Editor with his inexorable laws of space, does not stand in its way and roughly cut it down or expunge it altogether.'

A few weeks later Farrar was admitted to the Minehead and West Somerset Hospital where he died on 23 March. The *Free Press* reported:

'The day before, unknown to hospital staff, he made a great effort to write his *Notes* for this week's issue and completed about half a column, this being emblematic of the spirit of devotion which invariably characterised his work.

'His fresh humorous presentment of current events at once attracted attention ... he was a keen student of men and affairs, and out of a richly-stored mind, trained by constant reading and acute thinking, he could present things as he saw them in a way that always commanded attention and respect ... his mordant wit was feared by some, and seldom came out second best in a joust of words, but wherever he went he was soon the centre of laughter occasioned by some humorous of witty quip.'

Herbert Kille took over *Notes* straight away and wrote the column for nearly 40 years until his death in December 1962. 'He retired from active reporting in 1957 but continued to write *Notes By the Way*, well-versed and steeped in historical knowledge of the district. He died, literally in harness, for it was shortly after he had finished working at his typewriter and had retired for the night that he was taken ill. His father before him had instituted *Notes by the Way* and Herbert, on his return from the First World War where had been taken prisoner-of-war, came back to West Somerset and assisted his father in his work as chief reporter for the *West Somerset Free Press*.'

Jack Hurley, editor of the *Free Press*, took over the column in his own inimitable style until his death in 1983. Dr Glyn Court wrote his first column in January 1984 and for ten years entertained and informed us with his wit, local knowledge and erudition. My first column appeared on 8 July 1994.

I consider *Notes by the Way* to belong to the people of Exmoor and West Somerset and always welcome contributions, comments and, if deserved as they are on occasion, criticisms! I am grateful to everyone who has helped me with information over the years and acknowledge the work done by many other people who may not be aware of their contribution. Thanks particularly to Jeff Cox for helping sort out the history of the column.

Most of the photographs come from my own collection, given to me over years. If I have not credited where I should I do apologise and would be glad to hear from their owners.

I am indebted to Gareth Purcell and Sara Mace at the *West Somerset Free Press* for their support over the years and grateful for permission to reprint these *Notes*. This selection is taken from the years 1994 to 1999.

1 BEGINNINGS

The Youngs of Crowcombe

Old photographs have become big business. You can buy framed reproductions of your town centre in the 1900s, postcard copies of old views in the 'Nostalgia' range, while real old postcards change hands for several pounds apiece – and even more if an old motor vehicle is placed strategically in the foreground.

For the historian, old photographs have a different value. They are a modern type of archive, an historical source, providing evidence and information about the past.

Recently I was shown an old leather-backed photograph album. It had been picked up in a mixed lot at a house sale but had no apparent connection with the vendors or the house where it was bought. A cursory glance showed that the album was Victorian, the contents divided almost equally between views and studies of buildings in this country and on the continent, and personal photographs: school, college, the family and the family home in Crowcombe.

Many of the photographs were titled with subject matter and site but there were no personal names. One photograph taken in front of a window at Crowcombe House showed a group of young people with an older woman and dogs at their feet.

Who were they? Who had the album belonged to? Who was the young man who went to Bradfield College and then up to Jesus College, Cambridge and took idyllic pictures of cricket matches, May Races and a family picnic beside the Cam in 1886? I had to find out.

I began by searching the 1871 census return for suitable Crowcombe families. There were photographs of a croquet game at Crowcombe Court and a visit to Carew Castle in Pembrokeshire but no suitable members of the Carew family. The families of the schoolmaster, James Huggins, and of the curate, the Reverend James Boles, would have been too old by the 1880s – the tentative date that I had given to the family group. Perhaps they were the family of the vet, Harry Routley, who had three young sons and two daughters though the balance of sexes seemed wrong.

In the 1881 census I came across another family: Ellen M. Young, widow and fundholder, with her three daughters, Ellen (18), Nessie (12) and Katie (11) and son Bertram (8). I had overlooked them in the 1871 census because the parents had been away from home. Two other sons

Ellen Young with members of her family at Crowcombe House c.1884.

named in the earlier census were William Beardon Blamire (6 in 1871) and Henry Christian (a year younger).

By this time I had examined the Crowcombe burial registers and discovered that a William Henry Young had been buried on 17 August 1872, aged 34 years and 11 months. He was clearly the father of this family, a view endorsed by photographs in the album of the east window in Crowcombe church, dedicated to his memory. William Young left his widow, Ellen, with six children, the youngest, Bertram, just three months old. Three years later his eldest son, William, was to die in Brussels aged 10 years 7 months. He was brought back to Crowcombe to be buried and the officiating minister at the burial signed W. P. Michell.

I knew that William Philip Michell had been Vicar of Carhampton. Why had he gone to Crowcombe to bury young William? A search of the *Alumni Cantab.* showed me that William Michell was the son of a Cornishman, Bennett Michell, Vicar of Winsford from 1824 to 1857, and Matilda Euphemia, daughter of Thomas Wilson of Tobago in the West Indies. Ellen Martha Michell was William's younger sister, born in Winsford in 1842. The Revd W. P. Michell had taken the burial service for his nephew William, perhaps his godson and named after him as well as his father.

Incidentally, in 1871, three of the five servants looking after the Young children in their parents' absence had been born in Winsford; Elizabeth and May Emma Corner and Eliza Eyre. Although Ellen's father had died in 1857, she had clearly kept in touch with the villagers in the place where she had been born and brought up.

Picnicking beside the Cam at Cambridge, May week, 1886.

Ellen continued to live in Crowcombe House with her family until her death. Bertram was still living there in 1935 with at least two of his sisters and their elder brother, Henry, who had become Rector of Crowcombe in 1901 and continued until his death in 1943. It was Henry who attended Bradfield College; who went up to Jesus College, Cambridge sometime after 1883 and entertained his mother and sisters during May Week 1886.

And the earlier photographs taken in varied locations before 1872? Almost certainly they were taken by his father, William Henry Young, and illustrate his travels before and during the early years of his marriage. Who knows.

Four years later I was able to write a follow-up:

I always felt slightly frustrated that I had not been able to find out more about the father of this family and kept intending to try again when I had time to spare. Imagine my interest when I noticed in the columns of the *Free Press* a letter asking for information about the Youngs. On writing to the enquirer I was rewarded with quantities of information about the Young side of the family.

It turns out that Ellen Michell and William Henry Young were married in Minehead in 1862. Just what the Minehead connection was, I am yet to discover. William's parents were the Revd William Young and Sarah (née Blamire) who lived at Aller near Taunton. They, the parents, had both been born in Cumberland near Dalston, of farming families, and were married in Gilling in Yorkshire in 1830 where William's elder brother, Thomas, was rector. Thomas Young's wife, Mary, was Sarah's elder sister. The lady who wrote to me is descended from the Thomas Youngs and is lucky enough to have in her keeping a copy of a family diary kept by one of their daughters, Jane Christian Young.

William Henry had two sisters: Sarah, who died of whooping cough aged 16 in 1847, and Janet who died of diphtheria in 1860. They are both buried at Aller. Ellen and William had eight children in all. Twin boys, born in 1866, died the following year of diphtheria.

Several of William's relatives feature in a volume titled *Worthies of Cumberland*. His great-aunt was Susanna Blamire, 1747-1794, a poetess who was known as the 'Muse of Cumberland'. Many of her poems depicting Cumbrian folk 'with admirable truth' appeared in magazines although a collection was not published until 1842. She also wrote several songs 'of high merit' in Scottish dialect. Susanna's nephew (and William Henry's uncle) was William Blamire who was educated at Westminster and Christ Church, Oxford. He farmed at Thackwood Nook in Cumberland and became High Sheriff for the county and Whig MP for Carlisle. In 1836 he was appointed chief tithe commissioner and was instrumental in seeing that the Tithe Commutation Act of 1834 was carried out. This act, which commuted tithes formerly payable in kind, led to the drawing up of the parish tithe maps and schedules which are so helpful to local historians.

One of the most interesting points about the Youngs is that they originated from Cumberland. Both Joseph Relph (1784-1865), rector of Exford, and his contemporary Thomas Fisher, rector of Luccombe, also came from Cumberland. Was there a link, I wonder?

On the Cam, May week, 1886.

2 AROUND THE VILLAGES

Brompton Regis

Life in merrie King's Brompton

Among the many misapprehensions we have of 'those days' in the past, are the ideas that nobody travelled very far, that most working people in the country lived very simple lives and that there was much less crime than there is today and what there was tended to take place in the towns.

Working on these principles we might expect seventeenth-century Brompton Regis, or King's Brompton as it was, and is, known, to have been a quiet neighbourhood of industrious farming folk, all going about their everyday business with cheery faces and a friendly word for all. However, from the records of the legal cases heard at Quarter Sessions, that does not seem to have been the case.

Take, for example, the trouble Richard Venne had with his sheep in 1662. On Tuesday, 10 June, he left six white wether sheep, big horned, pasturing on Haddon Hill but when he went to look them over on the following Monday, he found that they were gone. Enquiring amongst his neighbours, he was told by William Sealy of Upton that Richard Woollcott had seen a man driving away six sheep like those that were missing, together with two lambs, on the same Tuesday evening about half an hour before sunset.

On further enquiry, Richard learned that six sheep, similar to the ones he had lost, had been sold in Dunster Market to Robert Hooper, husbandman, of Old Cleeve. Robert gave evidence that he had bought six big horned sheep at Dunster from one, Walter Pugsley, at about noon on Friday, 13 June. He paid 50 shillings for the beasts, which Walter Pugsley affirmed had been his own sheep, bred upon Withiel Hill. John Gaye of Old Cleeve agreed that he had been with Robert Hooper at Dunster Market when he paid Pugsley for the sheep.

Did Richard Venne get his sheep back? He went to Old Cleeve and claimed Robert's sheep as his own. We shall probably never know.

And what about Martin Ven [sic] of King's Brompton – the family seems fated! In evidence given before Mr Justice Malet at St Audries, he stated that on 20 May, 1669, Roger Clarke and two other men, whose names Martin had credibly heard to be John Stevens, otherwise Hawkins, of North Curry and Robert Holbourne of Dunster, had come to Martin's farm claiming to be bailiffs. They seized two of his cows on the pretended charge of non-payment of fines and amercements due towards the repair of the bridges in the county. Martin offered them half a crown to leave and not take the cows but they refused it and then drove the cattle away, beating them wildly as they went. Martin rode quickly after them offering more money in an attempt to get his cattle back. Eventually the con men agreed on a payment of nine shillings and he retrieved the cows.

Soon after, Martin heard of several other cases in and around King's Brompton where these same men had attempted to seize goods and had only released them for an exorbitant cash payment. Thomas Lyddon, George Hawkins, Richard Morris and Martin Ingram had all been duped by these rogues.

These are true stories, reflected in legal records. The frustrating thing is that we do not know the outcome of the cases.

Rather different is a tale set down in the 1920s in the Revd W.W. Joyce's *Echoes of Exmoor*. He wrote: 'There was a tradition of a battle being fought in the streets of King's Brompton, between the men of the neighbourhood and some invading half-savage tribe from Exmoor. All the old people of the place spoke of it in the early Victorian days and it is alive as ever as a tradition.

'The little army of rustic villagers were armed with reaping-hooks, scythes, coulters, pitchforks, and whatever implements of husbandry could be got together of a killing or damaging nature, while the invaders were mostly on horseback and had primitive firearms and swords and cutlasses. The slaughter was very great, especially of horses, and so many were killed that the blood ran down and filled the gutters along the little street. So runs the village story and the fertility even of certain fields is attributed to the number of horses which bled and were buried there.'

It is a tale which sounds as if it has links with the stories of the Doones on Exmoor. At a meeting recently I asked local people, some born and bred in King's Brompton, whether any of them had heard this tale when they were children. Nobody had.

Carhampton

Memories of Carhampton in the '20s

Recently I turned up this account of Carhampton, written down for me about 1995 by the late Mrs Ivy Hooper who was born and brought up in the village, and headed, 'As I remember 70 years ago'. Mrs Hooper's mother, Mrs Haydon, kept the post office in Carhampton for some 27 years at the beginning of the century. Her account recalls the village in the early 1920s, though occasionally it refers to things which happened later. I have augmented it here and there with information which she recorded on a tape at a later date.

Ivy Hooper with her elder sister Dora in Carhampton c.1916.

'Carhampton,' she wrote, 'has grown quite considerably over the past 60 years. There are many houses now where, for as long as I remember, there were green meadows and orchards. Orchards, especially, have disappeared and are now full of houses and bungalows and, of course, people. And where the old folk had an allotment on which to grow their much wanted potatoes for over the winter months, we now have a very nice council housing estate. I am quite sure the area would not be recognised now by anyone who had left the village even only 50 years ago.

'The village could also boast of five farms, two of which you could always go to and buy as much cream and milk (and butter) as you wanted. (These were Townsend Farm where Mr Watts farmed and Eastern Farm farmed by Mr Strong.) There were two blacksmiths; one at the top of the High Street and the other near the church. There were two carpenters, the workshop of one adjoining the (old) shop nearest the school and the other situated a little distance down Sea Lane, and there were two houses where you could purchase good china. There were two shops where everything needed was stocked. (One of these, on the site of the present shop, was Manning and Vickery which sold practically everything including groceries, dress material, sheets, underclothes, haberdashery and hardware).

'Some years ago, the post office was at the shop nearest the school (now closed); just post office business, papers and a few sundries. There was a phone cabinet inside for the use of the public and the mail would arrive by van from Taunton about 6am when, just after, the postman would arrive to sort the letters for Carhampton, Withycombe and Rodhuish. He was assisted by the postmistress and would be on his way, by bicycle, to deliver the same by about 7am. (The post office business was taken over in 1930 by Manning and Vickery).

'Almost opposite (in the new house built on the site of the King William Inn) was a butcher's shop and in the High Street a bootmaker and repairer. And, of course, there were two schools; the Wesleyan school in the High Street and the church school on the main road. A fair number of children were taught at both schools but the Wesleyan one was closed during the First World War and the children transferred to the other.

'Carhampton has nothing of great importance to attract attention, except perhaps the parish church with its lovely painted screen and the peaceful quiet little chapel in the High Street. When the village hall was built, it seemed a great step forward, a place where the lads could gather evenings and where meetings and discussions could be held; an occasional whist drive and, great fun, a social evening once a fortnight. Before the hall was built, there was the Temperance Band of Hope meetings held in the Chapel schoolroom, a Bible class held in a private house and, of course, choir practice evening where the young people used to go.

'To go as far afield as Minehead, you either had to walk the three miles (or beg a lift on the milk cart) or walk to Blue Anchor for a train or you could hire a wagonette from people who resided at a house in the centre of the village; the owner would drive the wagonette and take you there and back. (The main road was surfaced with stone, no tarmac, watered and steam-rollered, and the village was very dusty especially in summer although there was little traffic.)

'Two old village customs were the wassail night held in an orchard near the inn, which many people attended, and also the celebration of the ashen faggot held on Christmas Eve. The farmer at Eastern Farm kept the celebration for many Christmas Eves. At the rear of the farm there was a large building with a huge fireplace at one end at which the ashen faggot was burned. All who wished to attend were made welcome and, from early evening Christmas Eve, jolly songs like

'Daisy, Daisy' and other old popular songs were sung; refreshments of sandwiches and cakes and, of course, the farm cider were provided by the farmer and spread on a long trestle table down the centre of the building and, when at midnight the church clock struck 12, the singing immediately changed to Christmas carols and the celebrations went on for another hour.'

Accounts like this are so valuable for helping understand the history of a place. Perhaps Mrs Hooper's clear account will encourage others to record their own memories, maybe on paper, maybe by word of mouth.

Challacombe

Miracle turns church into magical grotto

A few days ago I visited the parish church at Challacombe for the first time. I went with a friend whose family has farmed in the area for generations and who has known the church and nearby farms since she was a child and known them too, in the memories of her mother who grew up at Barton Town, next door to the church.

Searching for Challacombe in my original paperback copy of Pevsner's *North Devon*, I wondered whether I was thinking straight. I was sure that Challacombe was in Devon, but Pevsner didn't seem to have turned off the beaten track enough to find this gem. (He didn't find Rodhuish either which I think says something about his inclination for exploration!)

The church, dedicated to the Holy Trinity, is simple: just a nave with no additional aisles. It was rebuilt in 1850, except for the west tower, and restored again in 1874-75. The pulpit seems to be inaccessible, save through a door at the rear which presumably leads from the vestry. It is situated nearly a mile from Challacombe village and people still walk up to church over the field path. My friend's family were Methodists and, walking down to the chapel in the village, they would pass the Anglicans on their way up and stop to exchange the week's news.

The gate that leads into the fields is also the way to the moor and reminds us of the numbers of families that came from the farms across the moor, bringing children to be christened and the departed for burial. Within living memory, coffins were carried from the farms to their final resting place on the shoulders of young men who would bear the weight for a while and then pass the coffin on to others before running ahead to stand and wait until it was their turn to carry again. Only recently, a wedding took place at Challacombe church where the bride and groom walked over the fields to their marriage and then, with friends and family, home for the feasting.

W.G.Hoskins writes brusquely: 'There is nothing of any age or interest save the font.' I cannot agree. The interior of the tower of the church is a miracle, draped with luscious green ferns which turn it into a magical grotto. While churchwardens and diocesan officials may well be anxious about the 'fabric' of the tower, visitors have, for more than a hundred years, marvelled at this unexpected sight.

At the end of August 1904, Madge, who wrote a chatty column for *The Formby Times* entitled 'Afternoon Tea Topics', stayed for a few days with the Huxtable family at Swincombe Farm.

'On Sunday morning we walked through the fields to the little church in the valley. The bells were ringing and sounded so sweet coming across the fields. The ringers stand at the foot of the tower inside the church, and the walls of the tower are full of lovely ferns. Looking down from the east it is such a pretty picture. The day of the month is rung just before the commencement of the service. Very handy too, for everyone can find the Psalms then, without a flutter of pages at the appointed time. The font in the church is comparatively new. The old one is on the road side leading to Barnstaple, and provides a cooling drink for thirsty horses. A very nice use to put it to.' Since Hoskins thought that the only thing of interest or age in the church was the font, presumably it has been restored to its rightful place.

Although Madge found country ways somewhat exhausting, she still loved the area and determined to stay for as long as possible, resisting the need to return home for 'Lifeboat Sunday'. Instead she supported the lifeboat at Clovelly, although it proved a tiring day.

'It is quite an undertaking to get away for the day from here, if you want to go by boat or train. It was really hardly light enough to dress the morning we rose to go to Clovelly. I was so overcome by the early rising, I was obliged to lie down on the form in the kitchen. At 6am we were driven from the farm to catch a train. We went on that new toy railway [the Lynton to Barnstaple] that opened a few years ago. The train looked ridiculous when it came puffing in. The platform and the line are all level. It is a mercy the rails aren't 'live'.

'One can't say the cutting of the line has spoiled the scenery. For the most part it runs in a valley. I don't think even Ruskin would have objected had he seen it. Such a valley, with a few houses nestling in the hollow, the hills each side clothed in pines. In the early morning light, with the sun just touching them, they looked perfectly lovely.

'The clock in the Parish Church at Lynton struck seven as we walked through the sleepy town, nobody astir but the milkman and a few shopkeepers sweeping out their shops.'

Lynton and Clovelly

Straw hats steam into startled Lynton

Lynton c.1890.

Madge, columnist for The Formby Times, *stayed for a few days in late August, 1904, at Swincombe, Challacombe. One day they visited Clovelly.*

Madge and her friends reached Lynton so early in the morning that few were astir. 'They gazed at us as if we were from another hemisphere. I wondered if they thought we were the messengers from Mars,' wrote Madge.

The three young women were probably in their twenties and, coming as they did from northern towns, were doubtless dressed in the height of holidaying fashion: long skirts, ornate frilled blouses and straw hats trimmed with ribbons and flowers. No wonder the inhabitants of Lynton gave them a second look as they made their way from the station.

The girls decided to have a second breakfast in a hotel before descending to the harbour, somewhat fearfully, by the cliff railway. 'It quite gave me the creeps looking down the steep slope.'

As soon as the steamer rounded the point, Madge and the other passengers put out to sea in a little boat. 'There were only six passengers, all told, from Lynmouth and they didn't waste any time getting us aboard. We had to make a mighty stride just when the boat rode atop of a wave and then a burly sailor caught us and hoisted us up. How tired those sailors must be of

Clovelly c.1885.

clasping women. There are not so many to clasp at Lynmouth, but at Clovelly they took hold of us like so many sheep, and dumped us down in the boats, and hardly were the oars fastened in the rowlocks before the hat went round and we were asked to remember the poor sailors...'

The steamer had picked up 'hundreds of passengers' at Ilfracombe so Clovelly was soon 'simply alive with people'. Madge admired the little town very much, although she bemoaned the steep, cobbled street for her 'feet seemed to pick out all the sharp stones there were.' They passed 'the baker delivering bread at the doors, and dragging his

Clovelly c.1885.

cart after him, which consisted of a huge hamper on two ribs of wood, his horse a stout rope. A good deal of the produce is brought down in panniers by donkeys.' From the top of the long street, Madge thought Clovelly had quite a Continental air with its gabled houses, donkeys stepping up and down and the blue sea and fishing boats below.

Madge and her friends had an excursion on a much more modest scale a few days later. They set out in the morning to walk from Swincombe to Woody Bay, a distance of some four or five miles, the first part on rough tracks across the moor. They were accompanied by a small, black pony which was to help them on their way and, when they reached Woody Bay, arranged for the pony to be stabled at the hotel until their return. They made their way down to Lee Mouth, a little sheltered cove a few miles from Lynton, where they ate their lunch 'lying on a sloping bank looking out over the sea. It was a beautiful day and we made the lunch hour last a long time.

'When we got down to the cove we perched on rocks and watched the tide come rolling in over great boulders. It was a fine sight. How I should love to have dabbled about there when I was a child. There was the loveliest little cottage away on the hillside, standing in a garden, with hives in one corner full of bees. We had tea here under the verandah.'

Afterwards, they walked on through the park surrounding Lee Abbey to the Valley of Rocks and then to Lynton station to catch the return train. 'We finished up this day badly, for when we alighted at Woody Bay station it was raining fast with every prospect of a dirty night and the tramp back over the moor to Swincombe.'

They had the pony saddled and then set off in the teeth of the storm. 'Shall I ever forget that walk?' wrote Madge. 'How fervently I wished I could hail an electric car, a hansom cab, anything covered. I am sure our own mothers would not have known us – wet, bedraggled-looking objects, one sitting on the pony, the other two walking alongside, lurching into ruts every minute. It was like a miniature retreat from Moscow. For all that, I kept laughing every now and then, it struck me as so comical.

'We passed one man and saw two women during the whole of the long tramp. I had little brooks inside my boots before I reached home, which cooled my ardour tremendously. It felt so delicious to put dry clothes on again that we almost felt it was worthwhile getting wet in order to enjoy the blessing.'

Clayhanger

Relics of the old ways

We tend to think that having no village shop is a recent deprivation but in fact there were once plenty of small villages and hamlets that had no proper shop but relied on a series of travelling shops and delivery vans to supply their needs. Nancy de Chazal in her reminiscences of Clayhanger during the Second World War recalls that there was no village shop there, just a sub-post office run from a tiny front room of a small cottage. This sold only post office goods, some stationery and string. Everything else had to come from the nearest small towns, Wiveliscombe or Bampton, both five miles away.

Today this would seem no distance at all but then it was a real trek. Few people had cars and of course, in wartime, petrol was limited anyway. Farmers' wives, I suspect, would have done their marketing using a pony and trap. Others had to rely on the train. It was two miles to Venn Cross Station to catch trains to Wiveliscombe but there would be a long wait there to return. To get to Bampton meant changing at Morebath Junction Halt, and would take the best part of a day. No wonder people relied on the excellent service of shops that called.

The grocer was D.W. Dunsford of Tiverton who called every other week.

'We got all our groceries from him,' remembered Nancy, 'and when he arrived with one order mother would give him the next. As the war progressed the order got simpler, as one could only order the amount of goods one was entitled to on one's ration card, and foreign goods virtually disappeared. Groceries at the time were the good old-fashioned sort.'

One contributor to the Women's Institute's *Somerset Within Living Memory* remembered before the war, 'loose biscuits weighed up into a thin white bag; sugar in strong blue bags; cheese in greaseproof paper; absolutely super dried fruits; Diadem flour and Oxo cubes in lovely red tins (very handy for children's treasures).'

'The fishmonger came from Wellington about 18 miles away. He seemed to be anonymous, came in a plain van and would only accept cash, no cheques, but he was very useful because he provided sausages and bananas as well as fish (until bananas disappeared towards the end of 1940). He delivered on a Thursday morning and we ate the fish on Friday for lunch. Those were the days when Friday was still fish day, a relic of the old ways.' When I was a child our fish man, I recall, also called on Thursday afternoons.

'The butcher was closer, at Hockworthy, some six or seven miles south of Clayhanger along a winding lane. He came twice a week with meat and eggs – often duck eggs, which were a great boon as they were not affected by rationing and were good for scrambled eggs and cakes. The market gardener called every week with vegetables and fruit he grew himself on a smallholding near Wiveliscombe while the baker came twice a week from Ashbrittle, five miles away, bringing floury loaves and large soft currant buns that were good with jam and cream – real cut-rounds!'

Once a month Mr Mason visited the village selling paraffin, furniture and china. The furniture and china were a hopeful sideline, as it was mostly paraffin he sold. Nancy recalled that during the winter months when the evacuated school was at the Rectory they used 50 gallons a month. Just before the school arrived, her mother bought a large quantity of plain china from him, breakfast, dinner and tea sets, 30 of everything. There was also a man from Petton who came each day with newspapers in a travelling shop that sold virtually everything in small quantities. Just right if you had forgotten something important.

Hardware dealers like Mr Mason had vans like Aladdin's cave! Some had the tank of paraffin at the centre with shelves eight feet high all around stacked with crockery nestling in straw from cups to chamber pots! There were saucepans, tin baths, brushes, mops, cleaning materials, garden tools, rabbit nets, snares, cartridges, small oil stoves and wicks and all forms of chick-feeders and drinkers.

Another style of van with the paraffin in a tank at the rear had a flat top with a rail all round. The galvanised buckets and bins were stacked on top and the van had roll-blinds of tarpaulin-like material that could be pulled down in bad weather. Smaller items were carried in pigeonholes or hung on hooks all round the sides.

Before the petrol-driven van country traders made their deliveries by horse and trap or wagonette. I wonder who it was at Dunster that contributed the following to the WI book! Surely it was dear Hilda Parham! 'It was the job of the sons of the baker, butcher and grocer to catch the horses before they went to school so that they could be fed and harnessed early.

'My husband was one of these boys and one day he refused to catch the horse because he had seen it being ill-treated by the van driver. No one else could catch it so it galloped off up the hill. His father had to hire a horse for the rest of the week. The next Saturday he had to climb the hill to find the horse, which came to his call and stood for him to mount. The hunt was out that day and young Jack enjoyed a bareback ride with them!'

Culbone

St Beuno or St Culbone?

Oare, Culbone and Stoke Pero,
Parishes three where no parson will go.

The tenor of this ancient rhyme, presumably referring to the isolation of the three parishes, was not the reason for my being invited recently to take a service at Culbone. Oare and Culbone are 'between' parsons at the moment so I was helping to fill the gap and was both delighted and privileged to do so. I was given a lift

Culbone c.1880.

from Ash Farm, past Silcombe and down the steep green lane which runs first between high hedges and then drops through deep woods to the combe where the parish church stands witness to the Christian faith, brought here some 1400 years ago by Celtic missionaries.

Perhaps Culbone church's main claim to fame is that it is reputed to be the smallest church in England. There are other contenders for the title but none that can claim to be a parish church with nave, chancel and sanctuary and where regular Sunday worship is held.

The church at Culbone is dedicated to St Beuno but it seems that for centuries the knowledge of this dedication was forgotten. The original name for Culbone was Kitnor. In *Domesday Book* (1086) the village is named as Chetenore and in 1236 in the *Feet of Fines* as Kitenore; a name which seems to be derived from the Anglo-Saxon *cyta* meaning a cell or cave, and *ore*, the seashore although in Ekwall's

Dictionary of English Place Names, the meaning is given as 'a hillside frequented by kites'.

Soon the place became known as Culbone and it was thought for centuries that the church was dedicated to a St Culbone. In 1532, for example, James Hadley of Withycombe left money to St Culbone (and other churches) because he had 'been remiss at going on pilgrimages'. When in 1633 Thomas Gerard visited the area he wrote honestly: 'There is in the Parke here [Porlock] a Chappell dedicated unto St Culbone, a Saint I assure you I am not well acquainted withall, and therefore can say no more.' Until the beginning of this century, topographical writers and eminent local historians like Chadwick-Healey continued to refer, often without question, to St Culbone. But there is no known St Culbone and if they did question it was generally to wonder whether the name referred to the sixth-century Irish saint, Columbanus.

As far as I can tell, it was only when Dr Francis Eeles, the honorary secretary of the Central Council for the Care of Churches, turned his attention to the matter in the late 1920s that it was realised that the name Culbone was the equivalent of Kilbeun, the cell or chapel of Beuno. In fact many people scorned this explanation and continued to talk about St Culbone into at least the 1940s.

As is usual with the Celtic saints, the history and legends which surround the life of Beuno are hard to separate. Beuno was born in Wales in the sixth century and was related to St Cadoc the Wise of Llancarfan and to St Kentigern. He became a priest and monk and established a monastery at Clynnog Fawr in Carnarvonshire in AD616 which became a great centre for missionary work. Beuno travelled in Herefordshire and founded several churches there but whether he actually came to Somerset is a moot point. Perhaps it was one of his followers who dedicated the church at Culbone to his eminent teacher and guide.

Beuno was also uncle to St Winifred, whose 'virtuous parents desired above all things to breed her up in the fear of God, and to preserve her soul untainted from the world.' Winifred's father was the Welsh noble, Trevith, second only to the king in North Wales. Trevith gave land to Beuno to build a church and recommended that his daughter should be instructed by him in Christian piety. Winifred took a vow of virginity and later became a nun, serving God in a small nunnery built by her father and under the direction of Beuno. Later

Beuno returned to Clynnog Fawr where he died in AD642.

The story goes on to tell how St Winifred entered another nunnery and was elected abbess, and how Caradoc, son of the prince of the country, fell violently in love with her. When she rejected him, he was so angered that 'in his rage he one day pursued her and cut off her head.' She was raised to life by the prayers of St Beuno 'and bore ever after the mark of her martyrdom by a red circle on the skin of her neck.'

Another piece of evidence for the early establishment of Christianity in the Culbone area is the cross-decorated stone on Culbone Hill set near the old north coast ridgeway between Lynmouth and Porlock. Dating from some time between the seventh and the ninth century, it is incised with a ring enclosing a cross similar to designs found in parts of Wales.

Legend goes that the original site chosen for Culbone church was on the side of the hill towards Silcombe. 'There is a small Druid's Grove above the church to the left of the green path towards Silcombe and here it is said that an attempt was made to lay the foundation stones of the church, but as the stones were laid by day, so by night they were scattered [it was assumed by the devil] and ultimately the attempt was abandoned.'

He hit him with a hatchet

Culbone (or Kitnor) had its origins back in the Dark Ages. When the Saxons came to the area, they took over old settlements or built new farms and, by the time of Edward the Confessor just before the Norman Conquest, the manor of Culbone was held by the Saxon, Osmund, together with the neighbouring manor of Wilmersham.

After the conquest the manor of Chetenore was granted to the Bishop of Coutances and was held from him by Drogo, an influential sub-tenant who held parcels of land throughout the county, including the manor of Porlock.

In 1086 there were just two villeins, one bordar or smallholder and one serf living at Culbone: perhaps a total population of 25. Land under cultivation was very limited: although *Domesday Book* speaks of enough arable land for two ploughs, the men only have one such implement; there are 50 acres of pasture and 100 of woodland.

Susanna Everett in her article on the 'Domesday Geography of

Three Exmoor Parishes' (SANHS *Proceedings*, 112) concludes that the two villein farms must have been Broomstreet and Silcombe which are both mentioned in manorial accounts in the fourteenth century.

It's interesting that the farm closest to the church at Culbone, Ash, is actually in Porlock parish. Presumably the stream marked the boundary. Ash was also in the manor of Porlock and was mentioned before 1400. Whether the Philip de Asshe, listed as one of those to be fined for non-appearance at a Pleas of the Forest court held in 1257, lived at this Ash or at Winsford is not clear. But wherever his home was, he didn't have to pay his fine because, as the record curtly puts it, he was 'Dead'.

Back in the thirteenth and fourteenth centuries, it was quite usual for there to be several junior clerks or clergy in a parish whose job it was to assist the rector or vicar. Culbone seems rather small to have needed a capellanus or chaplain so perhaps the rector at the time was non-resident or in charge of more than one parish. These assistant clergy seem to have been quite a rowdy lot. Charles Chadwick-Healey, in his *History of a Part of West Somerset*, gives many examples of goings-on at Porlock and it is he who records that in 1280, Thomas, chaplain of Cattenor or Culbone, was indicted at the Somerset Assizes of having struck Albert of Esshe or Ash on the head with a hatchet and so killed him. Thomas had fled and so he was outlawed.

One of the first rectors of Culbone that we know about was Thomas de London who came to Culbone in 1333 and stayed just two years. It must have proved quite a shock for Thomas assuming he was used to the medieval bright lights of his home city. But perhaps he'd been out of London for a while and maybe he came to this isolated spot to escape his creditors for soon there were writs out against him for debts of 100 marks to Bernardino Dyne and Peter Bernardini, merchants and money-lenders in Florence, incurred while he was parson of Meriet, and another for 240 marks while he was in a Hampshire parish.

The facts were brought to Bishop Ralph's attention and he reported back to the king that Thomas had no ecclesiastical goods on which to distrain and said 'the benefice of Culbone is so poor that it is scarcely sufficient for a priest ... we could find no goods on account of the poverty of the said benefice.'

In 1348-49 the Black Death swept England, decimating the population, and even reaching into isolated rural areas. In just six months, a half of the beneficed clergy in Somerset died and this is attributed to the plague. Out of the 22 benefices in the Dunster deanery, 17 became vacant in 1348, including Culbone.

Three hundred years later on 25 February 1641, Andrew Powell, clerk, John White, Jun. churchwarden, John White, Sen. and David Mogridge, overseers, of Culbone, together with fellow officers from other parishes in the deanery, took the Oath of Protestation affirming their loyalty to the reformed Protestant church in front of the magistrates at Dunster. They then returned to their parishes and on 27 February all the men of Culbone assented to the Oath: William Mogridge, John Smith (als Widen), David Mogridge, William Baker, John White, Simon Mogridge, William Long, David White, Andrew Powell, Jun., Hugh Powett (Powell?), Richard Martine, John Baker, John Reinolde, John White Jun., Thomas Warde, William Smith, John Chilcote and Richard Dune.

Back in the fourteenth century, clergy usually stayed at Culbone for only a few years. There were eight appointments between 1329 and 1353 which even allowing for the plague was quite a number. It was very different in the eighteenth century. In 1694 William Clare was appointed to the living by John Fry and remained there, living at Parsonage, until his death in 1745. He was succeeded, I believe, by his son, also William Clare, who is reputed to have served the parish for 50 years as his father did before him.

So extraordinary a spot

In 1794 Richard Lock in his *Survey of Somerset* noted that Culbone had but seven houses and consisted of 80 acres of arable, 200 acres of pasture, 20 acres of meadow and 200 acres of wood. What a bare description of the glories of Culbone which was about to become a focus for visitors seeking Romantic scenery and forced to travel in the British Isles rather than on the Continent because of the Napoleonic Wars. In spite, or perhaps because, of its isolation and difficult approach Culbone, set in its secluded valley between wooded hills and with glimpses to the sea far below, was exactly the kind of place that such visitors were seeking.

When Collinson wrote in 1791 he eulogised the scenery but noted that one could only approach on horseback with great difficulty and even danger, 'the road from Porlock being only a path two feet wide winding in a zigzag direction along the slope of the hills and often interrupted by large loose stones and roots of trees.'

This difficult zigzag path from Porlock Weir to Culbone climbing through woodland that abounded in 'wild deer, foxes, badgers and martin cats' was the route that Samuel Taylor Coleridge took in October 1797 when he walked the fringes of Exmoor, his mother's home country, and found, near Culbone, a lonely farmhouse where he was able to stay and complete his poem 'Osorio' and where he began his unfinished masterpiece, 'Kubla Khan'. This walk was to become a favourite that the poet shared with friends. Later in the same year he walked from Nether Stowey through Porlock and Culbone to the Valley of Rocks with William and Dorothy Wordsworth while in the spring of 1798 he took the same route with the essayist, William Hazlitt. Coleridge found inspiration in the Culbone landscape which can be easily identified in a number of his poems.

> The hanging woods, that-touch'd by autumn seem'd
> As they were blossoming hues of fire and gold.
> The hanging woods, most lovely in decay
> The many clouds, the sea, the rock, the sands ... 'Osorio'

In 1799 the Revd Richard Warner visited Culbone in the company of a shoemaker from Porlock who had offered to show him the 'remarkables' of the neighbourhood and took him a different way, up Porlock Hill and over the top for some six miles before turning towards the sea, presumably at the current turn off near Culbone Stables. About a mile from the hamlet 'excessive thirst', he wrote, 'obliged me to enquire at an old stone cottage, about which I saw some cows, for a glass of milk. A squalid female figure, opening the door, informed me there was no such thing at the parsonage but that a farmhouse, about a quarter of a mile further, would supply me with a bowl of this beverage.' Warner was clearly surprised that this run down hovel should boast the name of parsonage and his guide explained that in days past it had been the 'rectorial mansion' where the incumbent of the parish lived and had once been filled with 'good things'. After following the steep path down some 600 feet, Warner came upon Culbone church and was so charmed with this extraordinary spot that he later extolled its delights in several pages of truly purple prose.

Ashley Combe House.

In the same year a new house was built at Ashley Combe as a summer residence for the lord of the manor, Lord King of Ockham, and when his successor married Ada, the daughter of Lord Byron, he brought his bride to a newly-refurbished Ashley Lodge. I imagine that it was about this time that the road to Culbone from Porlock Weir was made up. In 1830 James Savage in his *Hundred of Carhampton* wrote of the small grassy plain at Culbone, three cottages outside the churchyard and a road leading from Porlock to Yearnor which was now passable for carriages from Porlock-quay to the church of Culbone, perfectly safe and with grand and beautiful views.

The improvements to the road made it possible to exploit the coppiced woodland between Porlock Weir and Culbone more easily for previously the path had been so rugged and dangerous that 'horses with long crooks could not travel on it.' Oak coppice, generally sold when it had attained 20 years' growth, usually made between £5 and £20 an acre in other areas but it had previously been worth little in Culbone parish because of the costs and difficulties of extracting it. Some 40 years before it was the practice for the bark to be made up into bundles and tied with ropes on the backs of horses to be brought down to Porlock.

Savage writes, 'A respectable tanner, of the name of Giles, who resided and carried on his business at that time near Porlock' sent parties of 10 or 12 men into the woods during the bark season to rip the trees for which he paid the lord of the manor a shilling a man per day as compensation for all the oak bark that they could strip off. That respectable tanner was Mr Giles of Holnicote who heard John Wesley preach in Bristol, was converted and, together with Richard Jones of Carhampton, instituted the first meetings of the people called Methodists in West Somerset.

Cutcombe

Cricket and cornets at Cutcombe

I've recently come across the reminiscences of John Bennett who grew up in Wheddon Cross. He moved to Minehead with his wife in 1918 and was 82 when he talked with Herbert Kille in Minehead in 1938.

John's father was parish carpenter, wheelwright, contractor, undertaker and part-time parish constable in Cutcombe. He also did a lot of work on the Bouverie Estate at a time when Squire Henry Bouverie would often come over from the family seat at Cannington, Brymore, to stay at Raleigh Cottage, not the present Raleigh Cottage but an older house which stood on the same site. He was a banker, member of the firm Barclay, Beaden, Tretton, Ransom, Bouverie and Co.

John was born in the late 1850s. He started school before the present Cutcombe school house was built and had his schooling at a house, long pulled down, in the village. This was probably the original school founded about 1720 by Richard Ellsworth of Bickham. John's first schoolmaster was a Mr Holman but he remembered more about Mr Hamlin who only had one arm, but ran a night school which John attended to further his education.

John went to work for his father and when he was about fourteen was the envy of the other village boys when he became the proud possessor of a bicycle, a boneshaker with wooden wheels.

'You sat with your feet up on the fork like a tailor sitting on a board,' said John. 'The brake was worked by a string that you tightened from the handlebar.'

After that John progressed to a penny-farthing which he had seen advertised and had written for to London. This bicycle had no brake but nonetheless John decided to ride it down Cutcombe Hill on his way to work at Steart. He hadn't gone far downhill before his feet came off the pedals and, with no brake, he just had to go and went down that hill like a bullet from a gun. He passed his father whose hair stood on end as he imagined finding his son in a heap further down the hill with a broken neck. But John managed to keep going until he reached Sully and the upward slope beyond slowed him down. As he commented, riding any bicycle at the time was tricky since roads were covered with stones as big as one's fist.

A Penny-Farthing rally 1860-1880.

The Bennetts lived opposite the present school house and there was a toll-gate nearby kept by an old woman called Stevens. The toll-house was little more than a hut. The toll for a horse and cart was fourpence-halfpenny and many lime carts avoided paying this by taking a 'narrow old road' behind the Bennett's house which led to Watercombe; an early-day rat-run!

John was very musical and became a member of the reputable Bridgetown Brass Band in which he played the euphonium. The members of the band were drawn from all around the area. Bill Pearse, a shoemaker from Exford who played the cornet, was the bandmaster. William Darby of Winsford, a noted hill-country cricketer of the day, played the second cornet; Charlie Gill, a carpenter, played the baritone; John Bevin, tailor at Winsford, the bombardon. Joe Rowe of King's Brompton was another euphonium player; Tom Phillips, a thatcher, played the cornet while a man called Quartley banged the big drum and Michael Court, a farmer, played the tenor horn.

Court had a couple of horses and carts and he used to collect the band and take them to various places to play. They provided the music for club-walks at Dulverton, Luxborough, Withypool and Exford and once went to Haddon Hill to play at a big picnic. John also played the violin and was much in demand for local dances. At the time grand dances were held at Cutcombe in the schoolroom and people came from miles around.

John's father played the bass viol while 'an old chap' played the clarionet. Jerry Sayers of Dulverton was a violin player much in demand at hill-country dances. 'We couldn't do anything against him,' said John. 'He used to play things we didn't know.'

John Bennett remembered playing in the first cricket match that ever took place at Cutcombe against Exford on Cutcombe Fair Day in 1877. It was particularly notable because the Devon and Somerset Staghounds invaded the ground and play was suspended while the kill took place.

Those who took the field for Cutcombe included W. Baker who afterwards became a Wesleyan missionary and went to South Africa; J. Baker who was blacksmith at Luckwell Bridge who emigrated to America and W. Passmore, coachman to the vicar, who later went to live in Exeter. G. Green was the local policeman and R. Adams of Putham was a farmer's son who subsequently moved to Alcombe Cross farm. J. Williams was son of the saddler at Wheddon Cross while W. Crockford was, in 1938, the only other survivor of that game.

Not much time for jollification

John Bennett, looking back to his days as a young man in Cutcombe in the 1860s and '70s, remembered particularly the high days and holidays. Cutcombe Fair was an event to which everyone, especially the younger generation, looked forward. Stalls were set up all through Wheddon Cross with gingerbread, sweets, fancy articles, shooting galleries and so on. A noted man for gingerbread and comfits who always had a stall at the fair was Mr Radley of Dulverton.

The fair field was then on the upper side of Wheddon Cross behind what became Mr Melhuish's shop and house and is now Exmoor House. Hundreds of sheep, as well as cattle, were driven there on the morning of fair day. Farmers used to pay so much a score toll as they drove the sheep and cattle in and John was often there taking the toll. There was no auction sale in those days. 'Farmers had to use their own judgement in buying and selling and they would stand and bargain for a bit and then go and have a drink and then come back to the field and see if they could make a deal.'

At the time the Rest and be Thankful was not the only inn in the parish. There was a public house in Cutcombe village called the Carpenters' Arms and one at Luckwell Bridge, the Red Lion or simply, the Lion. There was also the Heathpoult Inn at Heathpoult Cross kept by a family called Pope and then a very small place. 'They did everything in the kitchen,' said John, 'where they served the beer and poultry scratched and ran about. If you didn't mind, the fowls would come up and take your dinner out of your hand while you were eating it there.' John does not refer to the story of Fanny Pope who once lived at the inn and was reputed to be a witch.

Sheep-shearing in the 60s and 70s were notable events. 'I could turn my hand to anything,' John said, 'hay-making, sheep-shearing and many other things. Sometimes a farmer would come and ask us if we would like to go and help shear. We used to keep on several hands and I would let two or three of them go for a week or two and sometimes I helped. There were two ways of sheep-shearing then. One of them was what you might call "gentleman-shearing" for which you didn't get paid, and the other was what they called the "taskers" who were paid so much a score.

'If you were gentleman-shearing you did a few sheep first thing and about half past ten you sat down for a while and had a drink. Then you would do a few more sheep and go and have dinner. You would sit down for a bit and chat after dinner and then you would go out and shear a few more sheep; then it was time for a cup of tea. And the gentlemen-shearers would finish up the evening with some singing and dancing. It didn't matter much to them about having to be up the next morning.

'But the taskers, they were a gang who used to go about from one farm to another at shearing time – would start at five in the morning and work until five or six in the evening. They would get so much a score for their work and perhaps their breakfast and dinner and immediately they had finished one job they were off to the next one; there was no jollification for them. Some farmers let all their shearing to the taskers and the biggest local shearing was at Kersham where they used to take taskers who needed three or four days, to finish the job.'

John claimed that he could turn his hand to anything and this claim seems to have had a pretty wide application for it included tooth extraction for John was a dentist like his father before him.

Teeth were removed in those days with an instrument known as a Fox's key made in the shape of a gimlet with, at the end of the rod, a strong hook which operated on a swivel. The hook was fitted round the offending tooth, the dentist gave a sharp twist and out came the tooth – if the patient was lucky. John remembered getting friends to hold the patient's head or, occasionally, sitting the patient on the ground with his head between his knees, holding it tight. There was no gas but John was always careful to get the hook round the tooth so as not to tear the gum.

Other events that John recalled were the celebratory bonfires on Dunkery which he helped build and the popular race meetings on Minehead beach. There long lines of stalls and booths crowded the sea-front to the eastward and boxing contests between local men, some from Cutcombe, all drew the young farm labourers and artisans away from their work and down to the races.

This sporting event is supposed to have originated from a wager made between Mr William Escott of Wheddon Farm and Mr Boucher of Rodhuish. Mr Escott was a noted man for racing and had some very good horses. Gipsy, Mr Escott's horse, and Nimrod, belonging to Mr Boucher, were the first horses to race for a wager on the beach and on that occasion Mr Escott's horse won.

Dulverton

Unpleasant if not improper proximity

There are relatively few parish churches about Exmoor and West Somerset that escaped the improving hands of the Victorians. Molland, Trentishoe, the old church at Parracombe, Rodhuish, all spring to mind as churches each retaining one or more of the prayer book features of pre-Victorian days: three-decker pulpit, singing gallery, box pews, the Ten Commandments and the Lord's Prayer writ up for all. But many others were heavily 'restored', leaving later generations to regret what was lost.

Certainly, some churches really do seem to have been in an appalling and dangerous state of decay. Take, for example, the parish church of All Saints, Dulverton. It was totally rebuilt, save for the tower, in 1852-55 by Edward Ashworth of Exeter.

Why was such drastic re-building necessary? After all, when Collinson wrote about the building in 1791, he didn't mention any problems but, then, he didn't say very much at all. 'The church of Dulverton is a neat Gothic structure, composed of a nave, chancel and two side aisles. At the west end is an embattled tower, 60 feet high, with a small turret at one corner and containing a clock and five bells. The fourth bell was brought from Barlynch priory. In the south aisle is an elegant mural monument of white marble, inscribed to the memory of Humphrey Sydenham Esq. whose least honour was his descent from an ancient and worthy family. The christenings in this parish are yearly 20, the burials 18'!

It does seem, however, that 50 years later there were sound reasons for the church to be totally rebuilt. Dr G. F. Sydenham, in a talk given to Dulverton Church of England Men's Society in 1907, sets out these reasons, stating that the congregation had long outgrown the old church which was full of proprietary pews, the private property of well-to-do families and which couldn't be altered, while at the same time the building was constantly under repair and upkeep was proving very costly.

The architect, Edward Ashworth, was called in to survey the situation and give advice on what should be done and his report gives more detail of the problems. In order to provide more seating for the ever-growing congregation, wooden galleries had been put up all around the church and in the process of doing this, grave structural damage had been done to the building. At the same time the galleries had 'darkened and rendered unhealthy the air surrounding the seats beneath them' and having a level too near the ceilings there was no provision for ventilation. The galleries obstructed the light and when, to remedy this, windows were inserted in the roof and north wall they were both inconsistent with the style of the building and insufficient for providing light and air.

The gallery built over the rood screen was entered via rough steps on the outside of the north wall and a mean door, set between unsightly buttresses that had been built to shore up the north aisle which was falling out. To provide access to the 'compartment' over the nave, one of the pier arches had been cut away but damage here, and in other places, was hidden by the galleries themselves. The lower part of the tower, which might have been used to provide extra seating, had been neglected; windows were falling to pieces and a large tree close by had been allowed to grow up and block out the light. The double benched pews were enclosed in boxes, some four-and-a-half feet high and in some there were seats all round 'obliging many persons to sit with their faces in unpleasant if not improper proximity to those occupying the opposite seat.'

In some pews there were fireplaces. It was the custom, Dr Sydenham said, for the parson to wait for the squire to arrive before beginning the service. One Sunday, the parson started up with, 'When the wicked man…', but the clerk interrupted, 'Please sir, 'e baint a-come yet.'

So Dulverton church was thoroughly rebuilt at a cost of just over £3,000 and was consecrated on 18 April 1855 by Lord Auckland, the Bishop of Bath and Wells. There was a congregation of 700 and the service was followed by a public luncheon and the inevitable speeches. Sadly, the remains of a beautiful medieval screen which Mr Ashworth had thought should be saved and restored, gilded and coloured at a cost of £120, was got rid of, but in the years that followed many gifts were made to the church to add to its beauty.

But fashions change and a guide book of 1900 states baldly: 'There is not much in All Saints Church, Dulverton, to rave about. It is large and commodious and when you have said that you have said all. In 1855 … it underwent a scathing restoration both inside and out. So drastic indeed was the process that the inhabitants, not in anger or malice, often speak of the church as new.'

Tall but true tales from Dulverton

A bolt from the blue

It was early in May 1827 that the tragedy occurred. William Webber, a farm servant aged 21, was killed by a bolt from the blue. The *Taunton Courier* reported on the inquest held by Mr Caines at Ridlers Farm, Dulverton. William had been at work burning sward with a group of other men on a field called Sanctuary Hill. Robert Hill, who had been working not three landyards from William, gave evidence. It was about three in the afternoon when he heard thunder, it became very dark and a few drops of rain began to fall. He saw no lightning but suddenly he was struck down. When he recovered his senses, he saw William lying on the ground naked and Robert soon realised that he was dead. The horse that had been working with them was nearby, lying on its back.

Seeing that everyone else had left the field, Robert set off towards the farmhouse to report on what had happened. On the way he met some of the other men and returned to what was described in the *Courier* as a 'truly wonderful' sight. William's clothes were scattered in countless pieces all around; some driven into the earth in an aperture two feet wide and others scorched. There were wounds to William's head, body and feet. The enamelled face of his pocket watch was completely destroyed and its machinery singularly twisted.

William had worn a remarkably strong pair of nailed boots, but some of the nails had been forced out and the leather ripped. No-one had seen what happened. One man working some 50 yards away stated that he felt his hat move on his head at the time of a 'remarkable flash of lightning'. The verdict of the coroner was that William had died by the 'Visitation of God'. The horse lingered in a state of torpor until the next day when it was put down, there being no possible chance of it recovering.

Down a halfpenny

The year 1867 seems to have been an anxious year for many Devon and Somerset towns. There was a 'strange feeling of rebellion in the air' linked with low wages, poor working conditions and the high price of bread. Fears grew of possible breaches of the peace, but they were generally unfounded. In November, some people in Dulverton decided to exploit this situation and 'for a bit of a lark and wishing to create excitement' circulated a report that a bread riot was likely to take place and that many people were coming into the town from surrounding villages to demonstrate.

Letters were sent to the sergeant of the police and others stating that there would be a riot on Tuesday evening unless local bakers reduced the price of bread. There was 'great consternation and serious apprehensions were entertained'. One baker became so alarmed that, on the Monday, he had bills posted all over the town stating that he had lowered the price of his four-pound loaf from eighteen pence to seven pence halfpenny.

Every precaution was taken to prevent a possible disturbance and, when Tuesday came, Dulverton was guarded by a strong band of policemen and shops closed early. So much for the 'lark' but while the police were in another part of the town a large crowd assembled near the Bridge and threw stones at the landlord of the Castle and smashed some of his windows. Was it all really just for fun?

Head over Heles

Round about Easter 1893, preparations began for widening Hele Bridge. The main reason for the widening was an accident which had occurred at the bridge a short while before. A coach and four was coming down Jury Hill when one of the drag shoes flew out from under the wheel and the coach drove the horses at a pretty good pace down the hill until it came to a sudden halt, stopped by the guard wall of the bridge. All the passengers on the top of the coach were pitched off and landed in the middle of the river, but fortunately no-one was injured.

When work began on the bridge, the water level was very low and what there was was turned from Weir Stakes just opposite Baronsdown, across the meadows at Machine Steep to a point on the river below Hele Bridge Weir. While the work was in progress, there were great opportunities for taking trout out of the diverted river in spite of visits and threats from Mr Marwood, the water bailiff. One workman was seen with his waders full to the brim with trout. The young men of Dulverton were fairly peaceable at the time, until the bailiff threw out a challenge that if they took any trout or eels illegally he would catch them. As you would expect, fish were then caught in plenty and one night some were hung out on the lampposts in the town and on the bailiff's door. Of course, no one was caught.

Well, the bridge was finished and the masons, F.B., W.T. and T.B. chiselled their initials and the date at one end of the guard wall. I haven't had a chance to look to see if the initials are still there.

Dunster

Dunster's hidden depths

When I first moved to West Somerset and began to take local history classes I remember that I was often regaled with tales of tunnels that apparently ran below ground for long distances linking, for example, Alcombe and Dunster, and Hurlstone Point and Selworthy. Although some of my informants assured me that they had as children entered these tunnels, I tended to be sceptical, feeling that such feats of engineering were, to say the least, improbable.

Perhaps the most often told story was of a tunnel supposed to lead from Conygar Tower to Dunster Castle perhaps linked in some way with the so-called priest hole in the King Charles' bedroom and the secret stairs which were said to emerge by the stables. I have always been particularly suspicious of this tunnel supposed to run under the town for nearly half-a-mile so I was surprised to read in a report made of a visit to Dunster by the West Somerset branch of the Somerset

Archaeological Society in 1942, that these hard-headed members had voted it a MUST to see the entrance to the tunnel.

They apparently thought it to be less mythical than most tunnels. The report states: 'From two quite independent sources during the past week have come versions of hollow sounds under Church Street when horses and carts pass over a certain spot: and it is significant that each separate witness described the .rumble or "hollow sound" as coming from one and the same point under the street.' Both informants attributed the sound to the tunnel which they had known about since they were boys. They claimed that it was one of the great adventures of their schooldays to wriggle into the tunnel where it started on Conygar with lighted matches or tallow candles, the best thrill being the hundreds of bats that dangled from the roof about their heads.

Several members of the party scrambled down to explore the entrance to the cave but as it was blocked with debris no-one was able to venture in to test the tale. Whether or not buses cause the same hollow rumble in Church Street today I don't know but I have always put down the possibility of a 'passage' under the street to either drains or water supply dating from the time of the medieval priory. If you visit Cleeve Abbey you can see the sort of thing I mean.

At Alcombe the cave that was the supposed entrance to the tunnel leading to Dunster was, I believe, part of some exploratory adits made in a search for copper, tin, lead and coal in the early eighteenth century. The searches proved fruitless but the entrance to the adit could still be found when I last looked, a few years ago now.

Talking of holes in the ground, I wonder whether anyone knows anything about a monumental memorial to a horse which once stood in a quiet spot on the edge of the village near Dunster Steep. The story goes that during the war the tomb was spotted on land leased with the Luttrell Arms Hotel by Captain Ailward Wyndham while taking part in a Home Guard exercise. The memorial consisted then of an immense slab of slate three inches thick on which was built an altar tomb of Bath stone. The supporting panels were skilfully moulded and the longer sides adorned at each end with columns and capitals. The covering stone and several panels were missing but one with an inscription had been laid on the top.

Once the inscription had been cleaned it was found to read: 'Nelson, My Favourite and Noble Horse, Born at Felbrigg, Norfolk in 1?40, Died at Dunster 3 May 1?56. S.W.'

At first it was thought that the tomb might date from the sixteenth century and refer to some member of the Wyndham family who once owned Felbrigg. More careful investigation into the style of stonework and the lettering, however, suggested that it was likely to be much later and the figures to be 1840 and 1856. During that period the Withycombe family kept the Luttrell Arms and for a while it was thought that S.W. might have been a member of that family. But apparently nobody bore those initials and the general conclusion was that the horse had belonged to a visitor, almost certainly a lady.

Subsequently the name J. Pearse was discovered, faintly carved on the tomb, and this confirmed its dating to the mid-nineteenth century. Pearse was a local builder and craftsman in stone who worked on St Andrew's church in Minehead and also created the Gothic and other architectural embellishment on what is now the Carlton Plume of Feathers [*now demolished*].

A correspondent at the time of the discovery said that, as a small boy in about 1878, he had been intrigued by the monument. He was told then that it had been set up by one of Dunster's doctors, a Dr Norman. Then the tomb was in an orchard about 200 yards east of the Luttrell Arms Stables. Was this where the car park is today? I would be very interested to hear from anyone who knows anything about Nelson's tomb or who would like to set me right about the tunnels!

Several years later I heard from Steve Cook of Brighouse with a possible solution. Steve's great-great-grandfather was John Bennett, hatter and woolstapler, who, in the late nineteenth century, carried on his business in what is now the Castle Coffee House in Dunster High Street.

Steve suggested that S.W. might have been Sophia Windham who was the wife of William Howe Windham (1802-1854) of Felbrigg. After her husband's death she is reported as making 'an extended tour of watering places'. Torquay, where she met her second husband, an Italian opera singer, was one of the places she visited. Steve writes: 'I can imagine that she might well have spent some time with her husband's relations, the Wyndhams of Orchard Wyndham and perhaps brought her favourite horse, Nelson, with her to hunt and ride on the Brendon Hills. Her father-in-law was Vice-Admiral William (Lukin) Windham (1768-1833) who fought with Nelson at the battle of Copenhagen. And of course Nelson was born at Burnham Thorpe, not very far from Felbrigg.'

If this were the case, what a coincidence that it was a Captain Wyndham who discovered and recorded the memorial.

Luckwell Bridge

Meeting room filled to overflowing

I received a letter, asking for information about Luckwell Bridge, from a lady who has traced her family surname, Luckwell, back to the parish of Cutcombe in the 1600s.

The hamlet is said to take its name in the first place from St Luke's Well, signs of which, a stone arch and a heap of stones, still exist. When Dom Ethelbert Horne wrote about holy wells in Somerset in 1923 he had clearly had little luck in finding the well but in later years Berta Lawrence, perhaps a more intrepid explorer, spoke of an old pipe of a pump and the well lying beneath a heap of stones in the field.

In fact the Bridge element of the hamlet's name is equally important. The settlement lies in a valley near a fording of the river Quarme where roads lead off to Porlock, Exford, Winsford, Cutcombe and thus Dunster and Minehead. Here are all the classic indications of a medieval, or earlier, settlement: roads, ford and bridge, inn to accommodate those needing a night's rest or who were unable to proceed because of the depth of the river, and a forge where pack ponies and ridden horses could be shod.

In 1791 a fair was held near this crossroads for the sale of sheep and black cattle. At some point in the nineteenth century the route of the road was altered to accommodate increasing traffic thus cutting off the main part of the hamlet from the inn and Long Lane.

Isolated hamlets like Luckwell Bridge tended to display an element of independence: a social group, a community which could make decisions and choose to do things not necessarily conforming to the wishes of the mother parish up the road. In the nineteenth century this hamlet seems to have been almost self-sufficient although many labourers would have trudged the converging roadways to their work in other parts of the parish.

Collinson, writing in 1791, tells us that there were only 12 houses in the hamlet then and today there are about the same number although some of the original buildings have been pulled down and new ones put up. But these 12 buildings provided all essential services for country people in the last century. The inn, the Red Lion, was kept in 1861 by William Poole and later, in 1865, by Robert Tudball.

The Baker family once kept the inn and a stone on the side of the extended house reads W B 1765, presumably marking the date of the enlargement of the building. On the old inn door, kindly shown to me by the present owners, are the initials TB and PP. Bakers from America claim descent from these Bakers of Luckwell Bridge and identify with the graffiti on the door. Beside the inn is a mounting block and a Victorian letter box is set in the wall. Next door is the former blacksmith's shop.

Near the bridge over the Quarme stood the old mill house while a little way up the street the village shop provided everything needed not only by villagers but by local farmers who would come down from the hills by pony and trap to shop until after the Second World War.

Perhaps the best recorded events in the hamlet's history relate to the activities of the people called Methodists. Bible Christians and Wesleyans preached in the village from as early as 1810 and in 1849 the annual mission was held in a room 'fitted up nicely for preaching'. This first meeting room was built into the side of what is now Steppes Cottage.

By the 1850s the old meeting room had for some time been 'filled to overflowing' for special services; it had become too small for current needs and was 'getting into a state of decay' so in 1858 Oliver Veysey, schoolmaster at Cutcombe and local preacher, bought the meeting house for £100 and for £30 had it converted into a small chapel with a little gallery. It was used for another 25 years until a new chapel was built on a new site across the river.

The stone-laying ceremony took place on 19 April 1884, and at the morning service the preacher was the Revd R.B. Clare of Watchet. After the service a public luncheon was held and then the stone-laying. Memorial stones were laid by Messrs J. Phillips, J. Pugsley, J.T. Thorne, G. Burnell, J. Quick, R.Tucker Jun. and A. Steer, and the Misses E. Hosegood, E.K.R. Tudball, L. Steer and E. Norman. Miss Tudball was only three months old. After the ceremony there was a public tea attended by 130 people. The chapel at Luckwell Bridge was to be a lively centre of worship for many decades.

Nearly 75 years later the chapel was closed for a short while for renovations and re-opened in May 1952 at a ceremony performed by Mrs M. Huxtable who, as a babe in her father's arms, Miss Tudball, had laid a memorial stone in 1884. Gillian Melhuish presented a bouquet of flowers to Mrs Huxtable. The chapel eventually closed in 1974.

Stogumber Brewery

Ale a remedy for indigestion

It's a sad fact that although the old buildings which comprised Stogumber Brewery were not pulled down until 1973, I never visited them – perhaps because I just didn't know that they existed. Fortunately, Frank Hawtin, once of the County Museum Education Service, together with members of a WEA class that he was running, were so fascinated by the Brewery that they made an in-depth study of it and then deposited all the paper work, plans and photographs in the Record Office. Their work forms the basis for these *Notes*.

My interest was really aroused when I came across an invoice dated 12 August 1858 from Stogumber Medicinal Spring Brewery to Mr Popham for 35 gallons of ale at £1 6s 3d and a kilderkin (holding 16 or 18 gallons) at 13s 6d, paid for in cash, receipted by Henry Watts, of whom more later, and with a hand-written note reminding Mr Popham that the cask was to be returned.

The 'logo' of the Brewery was a picture of a peasant girl offering an invalid a draught of the renovating water from Harry Hill's Well at Stogumber. This well is apparently documented back to the 1400s and the local story is that a man named Harry Hill, suffering from a skin disease described in medieval times as leprosy, went and washed in the well-water and was healed. The well was named after him.

An article which appeared first in the *Somerset County Herald* in 1851 and was later published in a publicity brochure, tells the story of St Decuman, one of the first missionaries to West Somerset, who travelled from Wales on a raft accompanied by his cow (or maybe on an inflated bullock's hide). At Watchet he was attacked and his head cut off. Generally it is thought that the waters of St Decuman's Well achieved his miraculous cure but for the purposes of publicity we find St Decuman and his head carried carefully to Stogumber for the miracle to take place. A necessary advertising ploy, perhaps, when the water from this wonderful healing spring was being used in the brewing of an ale 'especially for the clergy and others with weak lungs etc.' and when it was suggested that references for its medicinal goodness and delicious flavour could be made to any of the Clergy or Medical Profession living in Devonshire.

The first mention of the Brewery is found in 1840 in *Bragg's Directory* for Somerset when G. Elers is listed as the brewer. It states that 'a large brewery has been recently established here by Mr Elers which has much increased the commerce of the place.' On 22 July 1840 the Williton Union Rate Book records that George Elers had paid his poor rate. By 1842, *Pigot's Directory* notes that there was 'a considerable brewing establishment here – the malt liquor from which is held in great estimation; it is said to own its celebrity in a great measure to the peculiar quality of the water, which is so well adapted to the process of brewing.'

The business seems to have taken off at a tremendous rate. On 1 February 1848, it was noted in the London *Times* that 'a spring of delicious water possessing medicinal virtues at Stogumber in Somersetshire, similar to that at the Cataract at Launceston in Van Diemen's Land, is now being used in brewing pure PALE ALE from malt and hops only, first introduced at Exeter in cases of indigestion, constipation and consumption through the advice of the Faculty, and now drank by the clergy, gentry, and most families throughout the West of England.'

By now Henry Watts was manager of both spring and brewery and ale was being sent all over the country to agents as far afield as London, Aberdeen, Manchester, Beccles, Launceston and Guernsey. The inhabitants of any town were invited to apply for an agent to be appointed in their town to supply them with the ale in small casks or bottles.

The casks of beer needed, of course, to be looked after carefully. 'The peculiar quality of the water renders it necessary that the cask of ale should be put on draught immediately, and by means of a vent-peg give it air for a few hours only; the ale will then fine down in the course of two or three days and prove most delicious.' Casks that were not paid for in advance were to be returned within three months to the agents or to Taunton Station or else paid for. All casks would keep sweet provided they were 'corked up tight immediately the ale is out of them'. A tremendous number of casks must have been required to supply all this beer but no coopers are noted in contemporary directories. Certainly there was a cooper's workshop amongst the brewery buildings and doubtless all the coopers were employed directly by the brewery.

In 1861 Charles George Elers is described as brewer and maltster at Stogumber but later directories refer again to George so it may be an error. Charles George Elers was the son of the founder of the brewery and a Major in the West Somerset Yeomanry Cavalry. In 1861 he was captain of Dunster Cricket Club and either he or his father founded what was virtually the first county cricket club – the Gentlemen of Somerset. In later life he became a prominent figure in commercial circles following his discovery of immense deposits of guano on some little known islands off the south-west coast of Africa. This find made Major Elers so much money that he became known as 'The new Guano King'. He died in London in 1899.

Their personal appearance was greatly improved

The history of Stogumber Brewery in the last decades of the nineteenth century isn't very clear. In 1861 Major John Sloman was living at Springfield Lodge and the brewery was run for a while under the name of Sloman and Brander.

In 1889 Stogumber Brewery was offered for sale, together with the West Somerset and the Tangier breweries in Taunton. The property at Stogumber included the brewery, malthouses, a residence and grounds, together with eight inns, public- and beer-houses at Shurton, Stowey, Roadwater, Washford, Bampton and Barnstaple. In spite of the auctioneer's fulsome commendation of the famous medicinal qualities of Stogumber Ale, considered to be the best in London, not a single bid was made for the brewery.

In 1891 it was on the market again this time with steam machinery, arched cellarage, three malthouses and stores, as well as the residence and stabling. It was knocked down to Mr Thomas Starkey for £1650.

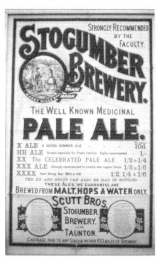

In 1893 it was noted in the *West Somerset Free Press* that a club had been formed at Stogumber to promote the drinking of Stogumber beer. The good conduct of the club was guaranteed by the 'very respectable committee' appointed to manage it. The reason for the enterprise was that all of the other public houses in the parish were tied to outside brewers and recently Stogumber Brewery had been re-opened and beer was being brewed on the spot.

Poster for Stoghumber Pale Ale.

By 1894 the brewery had been taken over by Messrs Scutt Bros, Ernest and George Decimus, who are described in *Kelly's Directory* as barley factors, wine and spirit importers, hop merchants and manufacturers of aerated waters which included ginger beer, lemonade, orange champagne, kola champagne (made from the kola nut), potash water, etc. together with a stimulating non-alcoholic beverage known as Winter Cheer.

But it was Stogumber Ale that was still at the heart of the business being brewed expressly for the clergy, Members of Parliament, public singers and people with weak lungs and Scutt Bros, relying heavily on the success of the ale some forty years earlier, produced a publicity brochure including scientific testimonials and Latin verses. According to the leaflet 'few Ladies and Gentlemen, comparatively speaking, drank Ale in England until this renovating water was discovered. Now thousands of the aristocracy partake of it as their only fermented liquor. Around Exeter where it was first introduced, it is now fully admitted that the personal appearance of the Ladies and Gentleman is greatly improved.'

The robust drank it for its delicious taste while the weakly were offered dietary advice to assist them in the rapid restoration of health.

Breakfast: a broiled mutton chop, a small quantity of home-made bread, one cup of coffee or tea made with soft water, with good sweet cream, and an egg boiled for two to three minutes – may finish with orange marmalade.

Lunch: Hot mutton, a small piece of bread and one-third of a pint of the Ale after the meal.

Dinner: Venison, mutton or beef, and bread, no vegetables, no pastry, no wine or spirits, half to three-quarters of a pint of the Ale.

Tea: One cup of tea or coffee with good cream, and home-made bread in moderation with butter or cream.

Elderly people find that a little ale taken with supper ensures a good night's rest but young people may find the tonic too powerful when taken at night.

The brochure also included a grateful 'effusion from one whose health has been greatly benefited by the use of the Stogumber Medicinal Pale Ale.' It is particularly memorable for the choice of words to rhyme with Stogumber!

Stay, Reader! stay a little while,
Whilst Fifty thou canst scarcely number,
And read pourtray'd in homely style,
The praise and virtues of Stogumber.

Go search the kingdom thro' and through,
From Royal Thames to Northern Humber,
No Ale, or Porter man can brew,
Will bear the prize from bright Stogumber.

Ye Cider Sellers, hide your Head,
Rejoice each painter and each Plumber,
You all who dabble much in Lead,
May safely quaff the pure Stogumber.

Does pain of Mind or pain of body
Weigh you down and banish slumber;
Fly from Brandy – Gin – or Toddy,
But take a glass of rich Stogumber.

Do Aching Thighs (whene'er you move,)
And stiffening joints, your walk encumber,
Would you move brisk? then haste and prove,
The strengthening power of pure Stogumber.

But one month since my legs were lank,
Each Rib with ease I then could number,
But now I'm plump, and how? – I drank,
Each day a pint of pale Stogumber.

While the scale of publicity was beyond criticism, the organisation of the business was not. A handful of letters from about 1899 complain of inaccurate invoices referring to goods already paid for or not ordered. But certainly the clergy did drink Pale Stogumber; there is an order from Mr Meade-King at Monksilver Rectory and I believe that Charles Howard Tripp, son of the Revd John Tripp, vicar of Carhampton and later rector of Sampford Brett, was manager of the brewery for a while before becoming managing director of Ind Coope & Co. at Burton-on-Trent.

Among these few surviving documents is a very elegant order, placed on 24 February 1895, by James Vicary of Carhampton, the licensee of the Butchers Arms and of the Kings Arms at Withycombe. Half a hogshead of common ale with the barm was ordered for Carhampton and 36 (bottles?) of common ale for Withycombe.

The disappearing pony and trap

However great the medicinal powers of Stogumber Pale Ale it did not make much headway into the twentieth century. By 1902 Scutt Bros. had given up the business and the brewery buildings and residence had been bought by Alfred L. Brandon who continued to own the property until the end of the twenties.

Brandon was described as a maltster but as far as we know little beer was brewed in the early part of the century although, in the 1970s, a Mr Bryant remembered delivering a weak or watered beer commonly known as bunker and retailing at 10d a gallon, to farmers in the Minehead area, the Brendons and as far afield as Bridgwater, who had run out of cider for their workmen. It sounds a pretty poor substitute! Mr Bryant drove a trap pulled by a horse named General who had that happy ability of always being able to find his own way home – very useful if his driver had partaken too liberally of cider or bunker! Mr Bryant recalled hops being imported from Kent but whether this was in the time of Mr Brandon, I'm not sure.

A photograph taken round about this time shows the rambling wooden buildings with a walkway linking the top storeys so that barley and other materials could be trundled between the malthouse and the brewery proper. There are 11 workmen in the photograph including Mr Larcombe, the cooper, whose work at this time was simply to repair barrels. Wages were around 14s a week.

When I visited Mr Fred Hutchings he told me that he remembered visiting the buildings as a lad with his father, Percy Hutchings. In 1909 Percy, who came from Williton, started up his own butcher's business in Stogumber leasing premises from the White Horse Inn; the buildings where the skittle alley stands today. Besides the shop he rented stabling for two ponies and a shed for the trap and he employed a boy to assist him. Percy lodged in the hotel during the week and the cost of all his out-goings – full board for five days, rent and the boy's wages – amounted to just 17s 6d a week.

Percy was one of that group of musicians at Williton often mentioned to me. He was both a talented church organist and a fine pianist, much sought after for dances and Fred remembers him setting off from home in top hat and tails to play for the Lysaghts at Old Cleeve, at Nettlecombe Court and at Triscombe.

Percy recalled that at about the time he set up shop in Stogumber, the main work at the brewery was milling feed-stuffs for animals. Later Percy married Ellen James and they went to live in Stogumber where their seven children were born. Fred, the eldest, remembers walks with his father and older brothers and sisters to the brewery in the mid-1920s. It was obviously an enthralling place for youngsters to explore. Fred recalls the great cellars with ten or twelve steps leading down and slopes on either side up which the beer was hauled by a windlass. He also remembers well a tale, current in Stogumber when he was a boy, of how a visitor had come to the brewery and, leaving his pony and trap in the yard, went in to the office. When he came out the yard was empty. Two of the lads had used straps to transport both pony and trap down into the cellars.

Once brewing had ceased the old buildings had potential for a variety of uses. For many years at the beginning of the century band practice was held in the loft above the wagon shed while later on the great 40-yard-long cellars became home to the Stogumber Rifle Club. Fred Hutchings remembers those days when there was a West Somerset Rifle League and teams competing from Williton, Old Cleeve, Dunster and Crowcombe as well as Stogumber. The police at Minehead entered a team as did Bicknoller whose open-air home range was in a quarry which made hitting the target difficult in windy weather.

During the Second World War the residence at the brewery, Springfield House, was requisitioned as a hostel for Land Army girls and I understand that there are today several of the 'girls' still living in the area who were accommodated there as well as 'lads' who remember going there for dances.

The water supply at the house came, of course, from Harry Hill's well, the clear spring water that had been the source of all the medicinal goodness in 'pure Stogumber'. When the land girls moved in, the water was tested and found to be 'unfit for drinking' and so Springfield House was put on the mains. To add insult to injury, after the war, the owners of the property were sent a bill charging them for this privilege.

Watchet

Watchet's living tradition

I was privileged to attend an annual meeting of Watchet Court Leet as the speaker. It was an occasion of great interest – the formal and traditional procedure forming an historic link with the first courts that governed the town over 1000 years ago.

In the tenth century the Saxon town of Watchet stood with its defences and its mint on the hill near Daw's Castle. Later, to escape the inroads of the sea, the church and town were moved to safer sites but the townsfolk took with them their ancient rights and privileges. By 1225 the town had become independent of the royal hundred of Williton and in 1243 was recorded as being a borough. By the latter part of the thirteenth century the townsfolk were governing themselves through two officials known as reeves who administered the borough through a court. The first records of this court date from 1273 and then survive for a number of different dates from the fifteenth century until 1606 and then from 1620 up to the present day.

Back in 1273 the court met every three weeks and the reeves heard cases of debt and trespass brought to the court by Watchet folk. They also ensured that Watchet-brewed ale was up to the legal strength.

By the fifteenth century things had changed. As early as 1350 the court was no longer run by the people but had become the property of the great family of Fitzurse. By the late 1400s the court was being held seven times a year and the lords of the borough, the Hadleys and the Fulfords, were able to make themselves quite an income from fines imposed on offenders, market stall rentals and charges for using the borough's bushell measure for goods coming into the port.

By the end of the 1400s the court, now known as the courtleet, was meeting twice a year and dealing with breaches of the peace. These were in the hands of the constable who, at a court in 1471, presented three Watchet people who had set upon Henry Irishman, one with a bill [hook], the second with a dagger and the third with a sword. Several brewers were reported by the aletaster for weak beer but local bakers must have been doing better for the breadweighers had no complaints. The twelve jurors were sworn in and agreed with everything done so far but reported John Ewayn, a miller, who had taken too much toll, and complained about a road to Dunster that was overgrown and of several straying animals. The officers appointed for the following year included two constables, two ale tasters and a bread weigher. The court fined John Hosyer and Robert Gray, already in trouble for hitting Henry Irishman with the bill, sums of 12d for making a great noise and disturbing the court.

Besides attending the court leet, the reeve had other duties which included collecting rents from the burgages (town properties), from fishing weirs, from butcher's stalls and tolls for using the bushell measure. But as trade increased during the sixteenth century these duties came to include control of the port and the reeve became known as portreeve. The work became more onerous and at least one of those due to take their turn at the job of portreeve appointed a deputy.

By 1710 Sir William Wyndham had become the sole owner of the borough and the court was held in the name of the Wyndhams as it is today. Sir William appointed a deputy to take his place as portreeve and, as he was often away from home, his agent presided over the court as is still the custom.

Sometimes there were troublemakers to deal with like Elizabeth Hearinge who assaulted Joan Hyker in 1629 and was fined for eavesdropping at night at the door of one of her neighbours. Round about this time the jurors reported that the pillory, cucking-stool and stocks were out of order and in 1634 they accused someone of dangerous driving in a cart. Another person was accused of abusing a juror with his tongue. In 1711 John Perret was reported as a nuisance for emptying chamber pots into the street.

Keeping the streets clear was a perennial problem. Sifting of ashes and winnowing of corn together with the practice of making dung heaps in the streets were frequent complaints in the eighteenth century. When the court met on 17 October 1717, the jurors proclaimed: 'We further Present that if any Inhabitants or Housekeeper leaves any Dung in the Streets above five Days after Notice Given to them by the Streete Keeper to remove the same Such Dung shall be forfieted by ye Streete Keeper itt being the Ancient Custom of the Burrough so to be.' Horses belonging to visiting butchers were another regular cause of complaint.

The court has met annually at Michaelmas from about 1650 and in the seventeenth century it was laid down that jurors must bring complaints before 2pm, in other words, before lunch. This practice continues and all business is over before the traditional meal of roast goose, apple pie, walnuts and punch, made to a secret recipe. Taken to each meeting of the court leet is the portreeve's staff of office, a long painted pole dated 1710 with Mr Wyndham's name upon it, a punch bowl and ladle and a pair of handcuffs lest any juror present some unruly Watchet person to the court. That didn't happen last week.

This article is based on research by Dr Robert Dunning.

Withycombe

Withycombe tales

Found in a collection of Withycombe photographs. Perhaps this sale of work was held in the Rectory garden, c.1905.

There is something compelling about exhibitions of village life put together by local people and incomers alike. In each one there are common threads: maps and papers belonging to the parish and held in the County Record Office, brought out and dusted down, old photographs, ancient documents found in cupboards, newspaper cuttings, and all enhanced by memories.

In the old parish records we can see the handwriting of our forebears as they kept the churchwardens' and overseers' accounts. We can see the names of old village families, entered meticulously by the parish priest as he recorded the baptisms, marriages and burials of his flock. Old maps and surveys record owners and occupiers of property, field names and even tell us how each piece of land was once used: arable, orchard, pasture, woodland.

Every time there is another exhibition more unique material comes to light as people realise the value of documents and pictures handed down from generation to generation. Withycombe has a tradition of such exhibitions and I know that on each occasion there will be exciting new finds to delight both local people and historians.

Looking through my file on Withycombe I came across an interesting little booklet put together in 1962 on the occasion of an earlier exhibition of village history. It is titled *Snapshots of Withycombe in the 19th century* and includes several interesting anecdotes collected from older people at the time.

Typical, was the custom at Dumbledeer of cleaning the chimney on Good Friday each year. The father of the family cut a young holly bush, tied a rope to the trunk, then went up on the roof and let the rope down the chimney. The children were waiting below in the kitchen and seized the rope. They pulled the holly bush down, bringing with it all the soot. Fun for them but not so good for mother!

Joanna Webber lived in two cottages that once stood at the foot of the church wall near the stream. There was no staircase and bedrooms were reached by ladder. She was old and lived alone, but sometimes had a visit from her son who was serving in a Highland Regiment. The village children were very puzzled when they first saw him wearing the kilt, not knowing whether he was male or female. One afternoon on his way home from school a village lad, Tom Burnett, then aged eight, saw her digging in her garden at the base of an apple tree. Being curious and thinking she was hiding some treasure, he returned later and found the hole covered in. When he was older and digging in the garden, he watched every spadeful for signs of treasure but was always disappointed.

21 December was known as Begging Day in the village. During their dinner hour the children visited houses and farms. 'Please, have you anything to give us for Christmas?' they asked. Mr and Mrs Robert Case at the Farm gave them a basket of apples as did Mr and Mrs Oatway at Sandhill. Some people chased them away with a broom, but old Joanna Webber gave them a basin of cold potatoes which they were glad to eat, there and then.

Eliza Hobbs kept the village shop. It was so dark that when Eliza wanted to get something from her store at the back she had to light a candle and grope in the corners to find it. She was mean and not much liked by the village children. On one occasion, when weighing up a pound of raisins, which they then called figs, found she was short of the required amount and cut an additional fig in two to make up the weight. After this she was always known as Eliza Cut-fig.

The mill was in regular use and Thomas Davey, the miller, lived at the Mill House. There was a large water wheel outside with the stream gushing down to drive it. The children used to go and watch him grind the corn. When the sack was full of flour it would be hung on a chain and hauled up through a trap door to the store room above.

Withies were cut in Combe Lane and woven into baskets by Jesse Heard who also made wicker beehives or skeps and travelled the area on his tricycle, selling his wares.

John Pearse was in charge of road repairs and would bring in a cartload of large stones. Jimmy Moore sat all day long in the lane cracking these stones until they were the size of eggs. They would then be spread on bad patches on the roads to be worn down by the feet of walkers who, in the process, wore out their boots.

Kelly's Directories show that these stories date from around the 1890s when Robert Case farmed at Withycombe Farm and John Oatway at Sandhill. Mrs Mary Hagley farmed at Combe while the Levershas were at Court Place. In 1894 village craftsmen included William Case, blacksmith; Jonathan Griffith and Charles Harrison, carpenters; William Griffith and William Pearse, tailors; Ephraim Hobbs and James Perkins, masons; Henry Pearse, road contractor and William Sully, shoemaker. James Vicary of the Butchers' Arms, Carhampton kept the Old King's Arms, Miss Mary Jane Hole was the schoolmistress and the Revd Robert Birtwhistle, the rector.

Withycombe Farm's threshing team working on the Brendons.

3 MINEHEAD

Minehead in the Eighteenth Century

The Ball Field and Hangman's Lane

Minehead, like Caesar's Gaul, was for centuries divided into three parts: Quay Town, Lower Town and Higher or Church Town. The three parts formed, as Savage put it in 1830 in his *Hundred of Carhampton*, 'an equilateral triangle whose sides are each about half-a-mile in length.' Separating the three parts were the remnants of the old medieval field system and numerous orchards. Writers of topography and of later guide books and makers of maps all underlined the tripartite structure of the town.

In the 1990s two missing eighteenth-century maps of the Manor of Minehead came to light. When I first saw them I was reminded immediately of a map amongst the Luttrell Papers at the County Record Office which shows that part of Minehead burnt down in the great fire of 1791. That map was reproduced in both Prebendary Hancock's *History of Minehead* published in 1903 and in Douglas Stevens and my *New History*. I had already discovered that the numbers on that map matched those of a Survey of the Manor of Minehead made in c.1757. The recently discovered maps looked so similar that I felt sure that they belonged with that survey and sure enough, on checking up, we found that they did.

The first of the maps shows the whole of the Manor of Minehead with field boundaries, street names, neighbouring properties and a series of dots in various places which I am beginning to think represent ruins. The second map gives three detailed street plans of the three parts of Minehead. Each building is numbered together with its adjacent land holdings. The accompanying survey is set out in numerical order and lists each tenant and property. It indicates whether the property is held by copy or leasehold and, if the latter, gives the lives and ages of those on whose lives the leases are granted. Between them the maps and the survey give us a detailed picture of Minehead as it was before the fires which destroyed the centre of the town and New Street, and add considerably to the knowledge we already have.

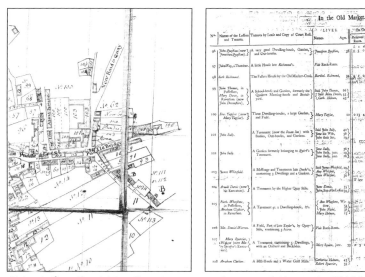

Extracts from the eighteenth-century map and survey relating to the Old Market in Minehead c.1770.

Take, for example, Thomas Tapscot who leased a tenement called Stotes. This farmhouse stood as it does today just above and opposite the east end of St Michael's church. Stotes is described as 'late Clothiers', an indication that previous tenants had been members of first the Clothier, and then the Stote families. Stotes and Clothiers were at that time living elsewhere in the town. The property consisted of 'a Dwelling house, Outhouse, Barn, and Garden; 2 Field called Clothier's Bench 1 acre and a half; the Green Close half an acre, Middle Bars and Little Close one acre.' The property was held on the lives of (I assume) Thomas's wife Joan, who was 42 and his children, Jane aged 10 and Thomas junior aged 8.

There were several buildings bordering the churchyard opposite Stotes and these included, near the lychgate, the house of the Parish Clerk, then William Stote. To the east of the church the road divided into three. Herring Shoot Lane led directly to houses tenanted by William Stote and by John Jenkins while Fishers Lane ran down across the fields towards the Quay. Bearing south down the hill towards Lower Town was New Street. This was a busy thoroughfare lined with houses which included a bakehouse and two inns, the Rose and Crown and a 'Brewhouse at the sign of the Ship'. Towards the foot of New Street Arthur Matthews and his wife kept a shop and just below their garden the lane opened out into the area known as Ball. From here a gate led into the Bowling Green. This had formerly been an orchard and seems to have been the only flat area of land on the side of the hill suitable for such a purpose. It bordered the Ball Field. It is interesting that the network of roads around the Ball established long ago has been retained despite all the new building.

A little lower down the hill near the present Community Education Centre stood a few scattered buildings which included the Presbyterian Meeting House. This was almost certainly the same building described in an earlier survey as belonging to Robert Saffin who held 'that old house at the south end of Folklands Court now new built and made into a meeting house.'

Middle Street began at the head of the Hollow Way and the whole area from there to the foot of Church Steps (then Church Street) and round to what is now the beginning of Watery Lane (then Hangman's Lane) was also known as Falkland Court. Here there were numerous dwelling houses occupied by some of Minehead's more wealthy townsfolk.

At the foot of Church Steps, Punter's Tenement was let out as the parish workhouse. This tenement included not only the corner house so often erroneously described as a jail, but also the house above as well as the one below now known as Pilgrim's Cottage. I was very glad to discover this for I could never understand how the number of paupers in the parish workhouse at the time (in 1810 there were 23) could have been accommodated in that relatively tiny building.

The Folly, the Wharfside and the Old Mermaid

Perhaps the thing that would surprise us most if we were transported back to Minehead in the mid-eighteenth century, would be the amount of open countryside between Higher Town and Lower Town and the coast. A painting of North Hill in 1735, reproduced in *Minehead A New History*, shows fields covering the top of the hill and sweeping down towards the sea. The recently discovered eighteenth-century map of Minehead shows that the artist did not exaggerate.

Besides those fields on the top of the hill there were others stretching from below the church and the Ball to just above the houses of Quay Town where the land dropped away and was too steep to be worked. Crossed by narrow lanes the fields extended right across to the Warren where the golf course is today.

The main route from the town leading to the harbour was the road soon to be known as New Road (and today as Blenheim Road) while Quay Lane linked Middle Street with the sea. At the foot of Water Lane (now the Avenue) was the Lower Quay stile and nearby a single house tenanted by Philip Sydenham and known as Blenheim. I am yet to discover why the name was perpetuated in a road a little distance away. At the junction of New Road and Quay Street were a group of large houses including a farmhouse, several malt houses and two coal yards on the seaward side. There was also a 'common oven'.

Many of the present day houses in Quay Street have their origins in properties shown on this map but there were far more buildings then than there are today.

Many of the occupants of the properties in the narrower part of the street were merchants or ship-owners. Their houses faced across the road to the wharfside where individual wharfs and storage buildings made up part of their properties. A protective wall known as the Wharf Wall ran the whole length of the wharfside.

Storms were a constant problem. One which blew up at Christmas in 1715 shattered the sea-facing wall, broke up the wharfside and demolished a number of houses. The following year the master mason, Thomas Chidgey, from Watchet, rebuilt the wall 'five feet at the bottom and three feet on Topp, containing fifty feet long and twenty feet high.' He had to obtain 'all material of lyme etc. and to draw the stones at Dunniford, and to bring them up Pitt to be loaded on the vessel.' Madam Dorothy Luttrell bore the expense of bringing them to Minehead. In 1741 another great storm beat down a large section of the Wharf Wall and several houses and more 'are in danger by the violence of the sea, and the whole street leading to the Quay is impassable.'

The map and survey show a number of houses in a bad state of repair. Rebecca Jeffreys lived in Want's House, 'part of which is demolished by the sea.' This house was soon pulled down and replaced by Lamb Cottage which was in turn demolished in 1901.

There were a great number of inns and ale houses in Quay Street at the time. They were doubtless needed not only as places where mariners might quench their thirst and old salts exchange tales of derring-do but also to provide accommodation for the many people who travelled to and from the area by sea. I am not sure that all these inns were in existence at the same time but their names all appear in the survey. There was the Old Mermaid, the White Hart, the Sign of the Three Sugar Loaves, the Turk's Head, the King's Head, the Star, the Fleece, the Greyhound and a nameless Publick House near the common oven. The only familiar name is that of the Red Lion but that house then stood much closer to the harbour than it does today.

Around the Quay itself were many houses, stores and cellars with lime kilns close by. Opposite the pier was a conduit, presumably a small reservoir providing a public water supply. Next to the conduit facing the top of the slipway was the Wharfinger or Water Bailiff's House. This was occupied by Mr Francis Williams who had been elected at the Court Leet and who was responsible to the Luttrell family at the castle for the collection of quay dues. In 1753 these were valued at £102. He also had to see that all ships were properly moored and that they did not throw their ballast out into the harbour.

Nearly opposite beside the pierhead was the Custom House where Mr John Short, the collector of His Majesty's customs duties, lived. John Short paid the annual sum of £15 to the manor for the privilege of holding this post.

There is a mystery on the map and that is a building shown as The Folly. It appears to have been rectangular and possibly a tower and it stood behind the houses roughly where the Red Lion stands today. It is not named in the survey, and just who built it and when and why, remains an enigma.

When Minehead was damp and smelly

Several people have asked about the maps on which the last two *Notes* have been based. The present owner has generously given permission for them to be copied and they can be studied in the Somerset Record Office along with the survey. A re-drawn extract from the map showing the damage done in Minehead by the 1791 fire and relating to this article can be seen in Hancock's *Minehead* and in *Minehead, A New History*.

Minehead's Lower Town grew up around the staggered crossroads where the town's four main streets, Bampton Street, Frog Street, Puddle Street and Friday Street, converged. Bampton Street, which was the most important road leading into the town, left the through route at Cher Cross and carried laden waggons and pack horse trains, as well as pedestrians and riders, to and from Bampton, Tiverton and Exeter as well local traffic from nearby villages. Traffic from the Taunton and Bridgwater direction may also have used this route, although local goods from Alcombe and Dunster were probably brought in by the lane that led directly through the fields and entered the town at the top of Friday Street.

All of this traffic, most destined for the harbour, had to negotiate the narrow streets of the town before reaching the New Road which led from Puddle Bridge to the quay. Local traffic from Higher Town and produce from the farms on North Hill came down narrow field tracks or the steep rocky Hollow Way into Frog Street and the town centre.

The area where the roads met was closely surrounded with buildings. There was no Wellington Square and no Park Street. The maps that have recently come to light suggest that there was the narrowest of gaps where Friday Street and Bampton Street met before the road bore to the right and opened out into the new market place. Even here there was relatively little room, for a line of houses in the middle of the road stretched intermittently from the market place to Puddle Bridge. The first of these was named, appropriately, Island House, while the next block included the market house where market tolls would have been collected and complaints heard.

This main street was known as Puddle Street, after the stream which ran open between the houses. It was crossed by Puddle Bridge near the Old Priory and then fed water into a large mill-pond (roughly where the hospital now stands) which provided the water to drive two water grist mills before running on to the sea. On the opposite side of the road, a narrow lane, Fields Lane, led diagonally out towards fields and the 'fennes'. Directly behind the houses was the Westerfield, still divided into its medieval strips. The house known today as the Old Priory was then leased as a dwelling house.

The almshouses in Market Place Lane are shown on the map but no details are given of occupants. Opposite stood some small houses and the stock house or jail. The old market cross, the stem of which still stands,

The almshouses in Market House Lane c.1860, mentioned in the map and survey extracts on p.54.

marked the site of an earlier market place, but just when and why the market was moved is uncertain. A house known as the Fuller's House stood near the market cross and behind it was a schoolroom and the old Quaker burying ground.

In Friday Street there were several well-built houses with stables, crofts and orchards. Towards the bottom on the right, next to the George Inn, was the Town Hall where all imported wool and other goods were supposed to be weighed and a toll paid to the lord of the manor. This custom fell into abeyance for a while but, after the Luttrells had spent so much money rebuilding the harbour, it was decided to revive it. Merchants from Tiverton, unaccustomed to paying the toll, made an attempt in 1716 to secure Watchet as the staple port where there would have been no toll to pay, but they were unsuccessful and at the time our map was drawn all imported goods were being brought to the Town Hall to be weighed.

At the town's end, a narrow road known as the Butts (now Selbourne Place) linked Friday Street with Bampton Street. Townsend House, then known as Kirkpatrick's, had recently been taken in hand by the Luttrells and was soon to be re-designed. Later on, it was occupied by Richard Cox, Mr Luttrell's political agent. Next to it, in the Butts, was the Quaker meeting house and some cellars, leased by Robert Davis, a prominent Minehead Quaker and leader of the political opposition to the Luttrell interests in the town. Further along was a malthouse and a building where herrings were once smoked.

Bampton Street itself was chiefly a street of dwelling houses, some large, with additional buildings and gardens, and some small. There were one or two small shops and workhouses and a small house and herbary occupied by Thomas Nurcombe. At the foot of the hill was the ancient mill complex, leased by Richard Bourcher and consisting of three grist mills powered by water carried in the leat which led from the stream above Mill Bridge. It was here that the disastrous fire of 1791 broke out which destroyed some 90 buildings in the over-crowded and doubtless damp, dirty and smelly town centre.

Nineteenth-Century Minehead

Clerk Lewry's rule – and ruler

History creeps up on us. The '30s, the Second World War, the '50s, even the '80s, are all history to our children. Only a very few people still living have firsthand memories of the period before the First World War, though they may be able to extend these with reminiscences of stories told them by their parents and grandparents.

So when I came across the reminiscences of an 86-year-old Minehead man recorded in 1927 I was thrilled, for his memories went right back to the 1840s when Minehead had hardly begun to develop into a holiday town and was still much as it had been two or three hundred years before.

John Moorman was living in Selborne Place with his wife when he celebrated his golden wedding in the autumn of 1927. By then he was the oldest surviving native of Minehead still living in the town. He was born at Higher Moor Farm, the son of Samuel Moorman who farmed there and the grandson of Robert Moorman who was farming at East Myne Farm and Combeshead

Making cider, reputedly at Higher Moor Farm c.1910.

Overland round about 1820. By 1927 all of these farms had been let go, their land incorporated in nearby holdings and the buildings allowed to fall into ruin.

John Moorman lived at Higher Moor until he was about 11 and remembered his childhood days as being ones of arduous toil from morning until night. He did go to school, but fairly intermittently depending on the farm work that needed doing. 'I went on Monday morning and stayed home the rest of the week.'

The school he attended was that of Clerk William Lewry who lived and kept his school in the white-washed cottage on the right at the foot of Church Steps. John Moorman described Clerk Lewry, so-called because he was the parish clerk and would have been responsible for much of the conduct of services in church, as a 'cripple'. That is the word used in the account but so far I've been unable to find out just what the problem was. Perhaps William Lewry had been paralysed by poliomyelitis but, whatever the cause, he lived a full, active and useful life. He drove about in a donkey chaise and had to be carried into church in a chair. Moorman recalled that when Clerk Lewry married for a second time he was carried into church on a man's back.

William Lewry conducted classes from his chair teaching the basic three Rs and not much else and if any boy misbehaved he threw a heavy ruler at him. He then commanded the boy to bring it back and if the boy was as naive as to do so he would get a wallop from the said ruler. With the bravado of memory, Moorman claimed to have soon learned not to carry back the ruler but instead threw it, once knocking the master's inkstand all to pieces. Lewry must have been getting on in years when he was teaching young Jack for, when he died in 1864, it was recorded that he had been a schoolmaster for 66 years and parish clerk for 60.

Higher Town, the area of Minehead around the church, was in the 1850s very different from what it is today. None of the villa residences had been built and the area was still farmed. Some of the fields running down towards the sea were still divided into landshares separated by the same boundaries that had divided the old medieval strips that made up the North Field.

Opposite Clerk Lewry's, at the foot of Church Steps, stood the parish poor house, used until just a few years before Minehead became part of the Williton Union in 1834 and the workhouse was built at Williton to accommodate the poor of the area.

The lane that is now known as The Ball used to be known as New Street and John Moorman remembered from his boyhood days the blackened ruins of many houses in that street that were destroyed in the fire of 1815. It was said that while the houses at the top of the Ball were blazing, people down in Quay Street were busy for hours throwing water on their thatched roofs, so dangerous were the sparks being blown down over the hillside. The fire was said to have destroyed 20 or so houses and Moorman remembered several other cottages which were allowed to fall into ruin and were eventually pulled down.

I have been asked on occasion why there are no pubs on North Hill these days. Well, Jack Moorman's grandfather told him that there were once nine inns in Higher Town. One was Lower Moor Farm which, 100 years before, was the Post Boy Inn. Another stood near the junction of The Cross and The Ball. The story went, and this must have been about 1800, that one vicar of Minehead would always call in to this tavern before church time and order the landlord to close until the service was over. Those who were slaking their thirst were expected to drink up and get to church.

More of John Moorman's Minehead

When John Moorman was a lad to the 1840s, the centre of Minehead or Lower Town was quite a different place. The Parade was still known then as Puddle Street after the stream that ran open through the street down to the sea.

Since the Great Fire of Minehead in 1791, when more than 70 houses, workshops and other buildings were destroyed, much of the centre of the town had been rebuilt. Low, plain dwelling-houses fronted by walled gardens lined the street and the old fish market stood on the site of the present Market House. Opposite, where Haywards's Bars once stood, there was an old inn called The Castle. People crossed a little wooden bridge to reach it; evidently a different bridge from the stone bridge outside the Old Priory, Puddle Bridge, which was painted by Peter de Wint in 1841.

Where Bancks Street and Summerland Road are now were fields and gardens. The Avenue was the Watery Lane, a narrow, tree-lined track with fields on either side. The tannery stood at the top roughly where the Regal is today. I have always understood that there was an old fulling mill on the opposite side of the road where the Methodist Church now stands, but this had probably fallen into disrepair by the time that John Moorman was a lad.

Apparently the track to the sea was little used for 'people didn't go down to the beach much then, at least not for pleasure.' There was also a better road for vehicles, the toll road, which followed the line of the present Blenheim Road. A cart track ran along the top of the beach to the Warren and all the bricks used for building came from the brick kiln out there.

One row of houses which escaped the 1791 fire was Quirke's Almshouses in Market Cross Lane or Almshouse Lane as it was sometimes known. Each morning and evening at six o'clock the bell on the almshouses, Old Nelly, would be rung and this set the time for the town to go by. The bell was also used as a fire bell. One of the almshouses at the end of the lane was slightly bigger than the others and here a dame school was held for a while. It is said that there was a big grandfather clock in the house and children who did not behave were put inside the clock case as a punishment.

Another building in Market Cross Lane, which stood where the side wall of the National Westminster Bank is now, was a strong house or lock-up known by older folk as the stock-house. Here the town fire-engine, an old hand pump, was kept and Mr G. Tudball remembered in 1931 tales of men who had been arrested and held in the lock-up. One smuggler shut up there was provided with money, perhaps to help him escape. His friends sent him in a coat, the buttons of which were sovereigns covered with cloth.

The area now known as Wellington Square was also very different and where St Andrew's Church now stands was an orchard. There was a little old drapers shop on the corner now known as Floyds Corner and further up Friday Street was a chemist's and then a coal cellar. On the opposite side of the

The Plume of Feathers, Minehead c.1880. The front entrance was later moved to face Wellingotn Square.

square stood the Plume of Feathers Inn. John Moorman remembered that the front door of The Feathers stood on the side facing down The Parade with a little bit of garden in front of it, something I'm glad to know because there is a photograph which shows this view and which I have never been able to understand. At the time, the Feathers was kept by a Mrs Yeandle and was the place where visitors to Minehead would stay but not the centre of social and commercial life that it was to become later. That role belonged to the Wellington Inn which in the 1840s was an old-fashioned house with a thatched roof and an annual rent of £14, thought hardly enough to keep the roof in repair.

The Wellington was the centre for the Friendly Societies. There were two in the town, one being the White Breeches Club, so named

The Wellington Inn, Minehead, where the Friendly Societies met c.1880.

because the members, about 100 of them, wore white breeches on their club walk. It was also known as Mr Luttrell's club because he used to support it. The members of both clubs used to turn out on Oak Apple Day, May 29, and would 'cut branches of oak off the trees and hang them up on the houses and people used to wear oak apples.'

The first two new-style houses that John Moorman remembered being built were in The Parks. At that time there was no Park Street and no road through The Parks to Porlock: only a footpath from the Baptist Chapel through to 'the back way'. Between the mill and the chapel were old houses and barns. The road from Porlock used to come down Cher and Bampton Street and that was the route that the stagecoaches took.

Dang-it-all Sammy's illicit trade

John Moorman's father, old Sammy Moorman at Higher Moor Farm, was a bit of a rough character and known as 'Dang-it-all' Moorman after his favourite expression. John does not mention his father's smuggling activities but a contemporary of his, 'London' Passmore, so-called because he served his apprenticeship in the building trade in London, remembered that Sammy was pretty active in that line.

Ships used to discharge their illicit cargoes at the beach near Greenaleigh Farm and the 'goods' were buried in the fields there. A good deal of the stuff was brought up to Higher Moor Farm and sometimes buried in Longclose, the long stony field that runs up the hollow below Moorbrake. On one occasion, a very large quantity of kegs of brandy and other goods were buried there and, in order to disguise the newly-dug ground, the men built a privy on the site. The excise officer came up to take a look around, but went away satisfied that there was nothing amiss. Another hiding place was an old hollow pollard tree which stood at the edge of the field.

These stories remind me of Thomas Hardy's tale of smuggling in *Wessex Tales*. He tells of a hiding place constructed under an apple tree. The whole tree, roots and all, would be lifted out, the goods concealed and the tree re-planted.

The cargoes that were landed at Greenaleigh were divided up and then distributed all around the area. Sammy Moorman was one of a network of distributors and one night he was driving a wagon-load of kegs of brandy to Porlock by way of Bratton. As he neared the village, disaster struck. A wheel came off the wagon and the load of kegs rolled off the wagon onto the ground. Fortunately, he was able to obtain the assistance of the local blacksmith; the wheel was quickly replaced and the smith squared with the gift of a keg.

The quantities of goods that were smuggled in and distributed were huge, if another tale dating from this period is to be believed. Isaac James, then a young man, was out with friends near Greenaleigh. They came upon an area where the ground had been disturbed and, on hunting about, found 600 casks of brandy buried in a field and another 400 hidden in a smugglers' cave nearby. James helped bring them in to Minehead where they were stored in the cellars belonging to the custom house on the Quay. Evidently some of the kegs were broached during this rescue 'and some of them got drunk'.

Another contemporary of John Moorman was John Knight who was born at Bratton in about 1837. He also attended Clerk Lewry's school in Higher Town, though probably a few years earlier than Moorman. His uncle was the carrier who drove the stage wagon between Minehead and Bristol and, when he was about 15 years old, John began to accompany him. Before he was 21, his uncle had died and left him the business which he carried on for some 40 years until competition from the railway forced him to give up.

The wagon used to start from the Black Boy Inn in Bampton Street, then the last house but one on that side of the street. Between the house and the town pound, still used occasionally to accommodate straying animals, stood a row of old barns.

There were two wagons which were kept in the wagon house behind the inn. One made the journey from Minehead to Bristol on Tuesdays returning on Wednesdays while the other went up on Thursdays and came back on Fridays. Their destination was The Three Queens Yard in Thomas Street (near Bristol Bridge, I believe) which was a busy meeting place for carriers. In 1861 *Kelly's Directory* for Bristol tells us that carriers' wagons were leaving the Yard for Tetbury and Cirencester, Wedmore, Mells and Frome and Nailsea, but Bridgwater and Minehead are not mentioned.

John carried both goods and passengers. All the goods for the Minehead shops were brought in by him while market produce was brought to the Black Boy Inn to be taken to Bristol for sale in the city.

The journey to Bristol was not always easy. The roads were rough and there were over a dozen tollgates to pass through. John Knight was a great walker and would usually walk beside his horses there and back. He remembered travelling through heavy storms with the snow up to the horses' bellies. On one occasion, he was carrying a load of gunpowder while a storm raged and thunder roared and lightning flashed overhead. There was always the possibility of being held up by robbers and so Mr Knight carried a six-chambered revolver and was accompanied by a Scotch greyhound. Once a man did attempt to hold up the wagon and steal the goods, but the dog drove the thief off, mauling him in the process.

4 PEOPLE

Mr and Mrs William Gratton of Rodhuish

William and Mary Gratton outside their home near Lower Rodhuish Farm c.1930. Left to right, standing: Alfie Gratton (son of Jack), Nellie Gratton, Fred Gratton, Ada and Charlie Needs; seated: Bessie Case, Muriel Case with dog Bonzo, William Gratton, Mary Gratton, Catherine Case and Jack Gratton. Bessie and Ada were daughters of William and Mary, while Muriel and Catherine were daughters of Bessie and William Henry Case.

Lives of useful but unremitting toil

When Mr and Mrs William Gratton celebrated their diamond wedding at Rodhuish in 1942 they looked back on lives that were typical of many farm workers living in the remoter villages of West Somerset during the previous eighty years.

William, the son of a farm labourer, was born in 1859 at Leighland while Mary Ann Langdon was born two years later, less than three miles away across the fields, at Culverwell in Rodhuish. They lived and worked all their lives within a five-mile radius of Rodhuish, though, like many other families in the area, William had a brother who, searching for adventure and work, not necessarily in that order, had spent time, first in the police force and then in the coal mines of South Wales before emigrating to America.

At school during the years leading up to 1870 when Forster's Education Act ensured proper schooling for all, William and Mary Ann obtained what education they had at 'dame' schools. William went to a cottage school at Leighland where he was taught by Mrs James whose husband was the station master at Roadwater on the old Mineral Railway while Mary Ann had her schooling from Mrs Mary Case who kept a cottage school in Rodhuish. Whether this was the charity school established by Richard Escott in his will of 1785, where poor children were to be taught to read and instructed in the duties of a Christian and where girls, in addition, were to be instructed in plain work, spinning and knitting stockings, I don't know. It may well have been.

At the age of ten, William went to work at Wood Advent Farm at a starting wage of 4d a day with no pay for working on Sundays. He stayed there for eleven years, eventually becoming a carter, before going for a while to work at Treborough Slate Quarries which were, at the time, 'a busy little centre of industry.' Then, yearning for a little more excitement in life, he decided to join the police force and went off to Plymouth for that purpose but his physical condition was not quite up to the required standard. Perhaps he just wasn't tall enough! Mary Ann, meanwhile, had gone into service with Mr John Boucher at Stiles Farm, Rodhuish.

William and Mary Ann were married at the Wesleyan Church in Watchet in June 1882 and went to live in Rodhuish where William took work as a carter with Mr Tyler at Lower Rodhuish Farm. When, some years later, Mr Tyler was gored by a bull and died of his injuries, Mr J. H. Norman took over the farm and William continued there until he was 70, working in later life as a shepherd. He spent a final five years at Jenkins Farm before retiring. After her marriage Mary Ann began to take an interest in the work of the farm and 'made herself very useful in all sorts of ways.'

Their sixty years together were, it was reported, spent in 'useful though perhaps unremitting toil.' It was the custom of the Williton and Dunster Agricultural Association to reward long and steady service and in 1910 Mary Ann won her 'long service'' certificate for 25 years continuous service with Mr Norman and his predecessor while, in 1931, William won first prize for over 46 years service on the same farm.

On only two occasions during their married life did they take a holiday, once spending three days in Bristol. On the other occasion William went to visit his sister in Bridgend for a week but I am not sure whether Mary Ann went as well.

Occasional high spots were William's visits to the Royal Bath and West and other agricultural shows, where Mr Tyler exhibited his horses, 'Paragon' often taking prizes in the hunter classes. In 1891 he accompanied 'Witch', another of Mr Tyler's horses, to the Races on Minehead beach where it won the Hunter Stakes.

Although William and Mary Ann had seven children, three of their daughters died in infancy. During the 1880s and '90s, school log books report almost annual epidemics of scarlet fever, measles, influenza and diphtheria in the locality and every year some young children died.

As Methodists, William and Mary Ann probably attended cottage services and sent their children to the Sunday school held in Rodhuish in the years before the Bible Christian chapel was built in 1898. Later they worshipped in the 'Tin Tabernacle' as it was known affectionately but on special occasions like Harvest, whether in the chapel or in the 'ancient chapelry of St. Bartholomew', they joined with all their 'friends in the district' in support and celebration.

Descendants of William and Mary Ann still living in the area may like to know that this information is based on an account in the West Somerset Free Press *of 6 June 1942.*

Richard Huxtable of Challacombe

Diary of a millwright on the moor

I was lucky enough to be shown, by Mr George Huxtable of South Molton, a copy of some pages from a diary or day-book kept by his great-grandfather, Richard Huxtable, in the early-nineteenth century. The original document, part of an old exercise book, was found in the 1930s in the rafters at Swincombe near Challacombe.

Fortunately, the person who found it was deeply interested in the history of his family and so the book was preserved. All too often, people are quite unaware of the historical value of old documents and so they get thrown out or burnt. It is always worth contacting the County Record Office at Taunton (or the Devon Office in Exeter) if you come across old family papers and are uncertain what to do with them.

Richard Huxtable, the eldest of five sons of Anthony and Susanna Huxtable, was born in 1770 at Bratton Fleming. His grandfather was a miller. In c.1795 he married Elizabeth and moved to Challacombe where they had five sons and three daughters. Richard soon acquired the leaseholds of several cottages at Challacombe and by 1818 was Lord Fortescue's tenant at the mill, although he did not work it himself. His second son, William, was the miller for some years before 1840 while his eldest son, another Richard, kept the New Inn nearby.

By 1824, we know that the elder Richard was working as a millwright and carpenter and his daybook for the nine months between July 1824 and March 1825 provides a fascinating glimpse of the daily life of a craftsman in an isolated Exmoor village in the early-nineteenth century. The book is written in an awkward hand and the phonetic spelling and use of dialect words, some now extinct, indicate a writer more comfortable with saw than pen. The late Charles Whybrow wrote about the Huxtables of Swincombe in *Devon and Cornwall Notes and Queries* (October, 1965) and included a translation of the day-book. He needed the help of the late J.F. Huxtable to make sense of the dialect. I rely on his text.

The first entry, for 1 July 1824, is 'Martinaw droing timber', that is, 'At Martinhoe throwing i.e. felling timber'. Two days later Richard was 'soying geat stof for Axton', otherwise, 'Sawing gate material for Haxton [Bratton Fleming].' Later in the month he was 'Hom moing' [At home, mowing] or 'Hom to hay' [At home, hay-making].

Richard may well have been the principal millwright of his day in the area, for his reputation seems to have spread relatively far afield. The day-book records visits to mills at North Molton, Shirwell, Lynton, Barbrook, Kentisbury, Bratton Fleming and Millslade at Brendon. In August, 1824, Richard made and installed a new water wheel at Shirwell Mill and during the autumn made new wheels for the mills at Kentisbury and at Millslade, thoroughly renovating Kentisbury. Early in December 1824, he spent a week in West Somerset, putting in chucks, dressing the mill-stones and making a new sifter for Mr Ridler at Porlock and also dressing the stones for Mr Baker at Selworthy (presumably Piles Mill at Allerford).

Considering how difficult transport on Exmoor was at the time (wheeled vehicles were only just making their first appearance on the moor) Richard travelled long distances to his work. While many of his simpler jobs took just a day, making and installing a new wheel meant that he was often away from home for a week at a time, staying in lodgings in the village where he was working.

Richard combined the work of carpenter with that of millwright. He felled and sawed his own timber using saw-pits at home and in South Wood as well as at some of the places where he was employed. He spent one day in November in Culbone Woods, taking out timber for Thomas Lee, and a day in January pollarding.

Carpentry jobs ranged from making and hanging farm gates and putting in a window seat and a new staircase, to making a coffin for Susanna Joans. It seems probable that the Parsonage at Challacombe was being rebuilt in 1824 for the curate, Mr Mould. Richard worked there regularly and tasks included putting up lintels, putting in joists, jointing and laying flooring and making and hanging doors. On the back of one page of the day-book is an estimate or draft account. Making eight windows and lintels, sawing included, was valued at £1 10s while making a door, derns and lintels, sawing included, was 17s. This at a time when the average weekly wage of a farm labourer was about 8s a week.

One unusual entry in the day-book raises interesting questions about Richard. On one page he has written: 'When our blest savour was in the garden of Eden the cruel Jews scourged him with thorns his flesh did neither fester nor rankle no more shan't thine Elizabeth Brayle. In the name of the father and of the son and of the holy gost Amen.' Was he regarded in the area as someone with powers of healing, I wonder?

Sydney Whitehead

He thinks he'll ride now!

Memories are a really important source for local history. At the turn of the twentieth century and into the 1920s and '30s, Clement and Herbert Kille, together with W.H. Farrar, carefully recorded the memories of elderly people and published some of them in the *West Somerset Free Press*. These accounts give us first-hand information about the area as far back as the 1820s: information that often would not be available from any other historical source.

The lesson for us is that we too should be recording the memories of older people, and all too often we know that we should do this if important information is not to be lost but just don't get round to it. I was fortunate to have talked to the late Sydney Whitehead who first visited Exmoor in 1917 when he was three years old. He had been coming to the area ever since and was amused that people often turned to him, a Londoner, for memories of Exmoor. In the 1980s he wrote down some of these and he gave me permission to use them in this piece.

On his first visit, Sydney, with his mother and sister, stayed in Porlock. He confesses that he can't remember all that much about this visit yet one or two things stand out. One of these was the motor bus from Minehead nearly turning over on the hairpin bend going down into Porlock. Porlock Steep, the little slip road dropping down into the village, didn't exist then for wheeled transport. All traffic, up and down, had to go round the hairpin bend. Sydney can just remember the passengers' screams when the bus lurched as if it were about to turn over!

He went on: 'We had a large hamper for our clothes. This was taken off the roof of the bus at the church and left beside the roadside. Mother was somewhat reluctant to just leave it there but was told, "That's alright m'dear. The carrier will bring it up to the cottage later." We were staying in a row of cottages up beyond the water wheel, with Mrs Knight and her daughter, Mrs Bargery. Naturally the hamper arrived safely, and when it did Mother had no key. This, however, had been noticed in London, and the key arrived by post the next morning. Incidentally, I seem to remember the water wheel still working as late as the 1930s generating electricity.

'A push chair had been taken to Porlock for me. Evidently I could sense when the gradient was one degree up from level and used to say, "He thinks he'll ride now" – a remark that has followed him for the rest of his life.

Sydney and his family went first to Minehead round about 1922. On the first occasion they travelled by train and Sydney's father took a bicycle with them, probably to give a lift to his young sister. One of their favourite spots was the deserted beach beyond the golf club. 'Sometimes,' he says, 'we wandered back forgetting the cycle. The next day it was always there, just where it had been left.'

The following year they went to Minehead by car: a Model T Ford. The journey took a while. After an early start, the Whitehead family stopped for lunch in Trowbridge. In those early days, the family stayed in Irnham Road and Sydney was always delighted when their visit coincided with the arrival of the fun fair on what is now Minehead

Football Club ground. 'I can still recall the thrill of seeing the steam traction engines arriving, with a string of trailers behind them. No beach for me that day! It was far more fun watching the trailers trying to get through the gate, though the family probably didn't enjoy the noise.

'Naturally the town has changed. Where the Regal is now there was a tannery which used to give off some strange odours. Then there was a little cinema in Bancks Street. Round the corner there were no Blenheim Gardens. There was just a field, with a hedge along the side of the road. Cows used to graze in the field. At low tide there used to be washing hanging on lines across the beach. The harbour was very busy in the 1920s and '30s. All the coal for the gas works came by sea and a steam crane was used to unload the boats. The coal was shovelled into big iron baskets, lifted out and tipped into carts or, later, lorries.

'I can still,' said Sydney, 'hear the voice floating up from the hold to the crane driver: "Loowerr a bit!"'

Arriving in various shades of green

Memories are inevitably subjective. They include the matters that made the greatest impression on us when we were young: events that raised the adrenalin; the excitement of visits to friends and relatives and those very special moments when our own parents recalled their high spots, their own history.

Sydney Whitehead had clear memories of shipping in the harbour at Minehead during the 1920s and early '30s. Then there were mostly sailing boats that brought coal for the gas works and for household fuel and returned to South Wales with pit props cut in local woodlands. 'The last vessel in the harbour was the *Emma Louise*, still working in the 1950s, but who ended her days, rotting away on some mud flat down Bideford way.'

Sydney remembered seeing one of the last steam boats at Minehead being sucked out by the tide. 'The hawsers could not hold her. Everyone was cleared away from the harbour. Then, when the rope snapped it coiled right up in the air, and the noise it made was just as if a gun had gone off.' In the '20s the lifeboat was just a rowing boat as were the fishing boats. Sydney remembered being taken out fishing by Mr Martin who was, he believed, the coxswain of the lifeboat. 'I caught an eel, but I felt so ill that it put me off fishing for life!'

73

'Minehead had a pier until the beginning of the Second World War. Then two sections were removed to prevent a landing by the enemy – or so the story goes. After the war the sections could not be found, so the rest of the pier was pulled down. During the summer season Campbell's steamers used to call daily and folk used to pour into Minehead from South Wales. There was a little railway running along the pier for moving the luggage.' The journey across the Bristol Channel can be very rough and Sydney recalled: 'I have seen times when one would have thought an hospital ship had arrived – the passengers being various shades of green. It was not unknown for nobody to be allowed back on board until the decks had been hosed down!'

Those were the days when no-one considered that they had had a proper visit to Minehead unless they had had a cream tea at Greenaleigh Farm. To get there one walked, passing the gas works and then taking the first hill path, and all the way – about a mile or more – there was a wonderful sea view ('When I was young,' recalled Sydney, 'it felt a lot further') and at Greenaleigh maybe fifty people would sit down to tea together.

'The best hotel in Minehead in those days was the Metropole, now converted into flats and the Hobby Horse Inn. Back in the '20s folks could be seen coming out for an after-dinner stroll along the front, all in evening dress. The Metropole was where the Indian princes used to stay when playing polo at Dunster. The hotel had a most interesting lift. It was not hidden in a lift shaft but was out in the open and one could sit in the hotel lounge, watching the lift go up and down.'

The band stand used to be on what is now Jubilee Gardens. Ivy Benson and her girl band were regular and popular visitors. Further along was the Queen's Hall. This was a very nice little theatre, with a repertory company during the season. Back towards the railway station was the Gaiety Theatre – the home of pure seaside concert party entertainment.

Along the seafront opposite the Beach Hotel was where the charabancs used to stand. They had chalked boards displayed to show where each was going that day. Sydney remembers some of the company names: Lorna Doone, Scarlet Pimpernel, Mascot, Pride of the Moors.

American Reo chassis were much favoured because they had powerful engines and Italian Lancias because they had four wheel brakes. 'You took your choice how you liked your thrills! Some coaches were good at going up hill while others were good at coming down!' During the '20s there were more horse hackneys lined up outside the station than motor taxis and the Plume of Feathers Hotel had its own station bus to meet the trains.'

I've received an interesting letter from Doreen and Sid Ward, of Washford, who thought that Mr Whitehead might be interested to know that on his first visit to Exmoor he almost certainly stayed at 4 Sunnyside, Hawkcombe. This row of cottages once belonged to the Pearce family who owned Porlock Tannery. When they were sold in 1949 most were bought by sitting tenants but the Wards bought No. 4. The tenant of that cottage was an elderly bachelor, Mr Hedley Knight whose sister had been Mrs Bargery and his mother, Mrs Knight – the people with whom the Whiteheads stayed in 1917. After Mr Knight moved to live with relations the Wards moved to the cottage. Sid Ward was born at Porlock Weir and remembered his Granny, Mrs Tom Ward (then Mrs Rexworthy) buying the wood on a rap of land up behind the little church at Porlock Weir. Selling the bark to the Tanyard paid for the wood used as firewood.

More memories of the Twenties

Sydney Whitehead visited Minehead and Exmoor regularly during the early 1920s and '30s and his memories are wide-ranging. Take shops, for example. He recalled that at the time there were very few multiple shops in the town – very different from today. The Star Supply Stores stood on the corner of the Parade opposite the old Plume of Feathers Hotel and there was Eastman's, the butchers. Boots came later, perhaps in the thirties.

Mr Potter, whose gentlemen's outfitters was in Friday Street, always served his customers in morning dress with a long tail coat, while Mr Newton and Mr Batchelor in their respective grocers' shops, were in waistcoats and spotless white aprons. Mr Ridler ran a friendly and efficient footwear shop. Bagleys were very good bakers and their name can still be seen, high up on the wall at the back of (the old) Tarr and Foy. There were little dairy shops to be found all around the town. Browns was a very exclusive jewellers. There was a lot of money about in Minehead then with the hunting and polo.

Laundries in the area at the time included the Allerford laundry at Brandish Street, the Minehead laundry, the Convent laundry and the Hopcott laundry situated behind the Hopcott Hotel. Does anyone know of a laundry at Luccombe? I have heard that there was one out towards Venniford and, of course, Dunster Castle laundry was housed in a cottage at Dunster Marsh, still named, I believe, The Old Laundry.

Sydney was always interested in transport and Porlock Hill drew him 'like a magnet'. There was action to be seen there all the time. In pre-war days one of the most amazing sights was that of a Foden steam wagon reversing the whole way down Porlock Hill. This was for two reasons. First, the hottest part of a boiler is obviously near the fire, which was at the back of the vehicle. Had they driven down Porlock Hill all the water would have run to the front of the boiler, with no

Porlock Hill on a very busy afternoon c.1930.

water in the hottest area – and probably disastrous results! Also the Foden only had rear wheel brakes and solid tyres. By going down in reverse the weight was transferred to the rear wheels and the brakes got a good grip. Sydney only ever saw them coming down, never going up.

One day while he was still at school, Sydney and his aunt decided to walk from Minehead to Lynmouth. 'We made the great mistake of walking up the Toll Road, thinking that it would be easier. It may not be quite so steep, but it is one of those roads that seems to be never-ending. Eventually we were out on the moor. It was a wild open moor then; no fields to be seen, and only the occasional motor. Somewhere before County Gate the heavens opened, with real Exmoor rain. There was no vestige of shelter, so we were soon wet to the skin. Luckily my father had arranged to meet us at Lynmouth, and drive us back to Minehead.'

Minehead used to have its own cattle market round behind the railway goods yard with a path leading to it in front of the cottages just beyond the Beach Hotel. 'This path was well-used,' said Sydney, 'for the Beach had an all-day licence on market days. The sheep and cattle were driven through the town from the local farms. Mother made sure she did not go out on those days.'

This was when motor cattle trucks were almost unknown. Cattle travelling any distance were moved by rail and there were cattle docks at both Minehead and Washford stations. The big market for the district was then, as now, at Wheddon Cross. In the years just before the war Sydney used to ride 'shot gun' to one of the drivers of Pugsley's cattle trucks. He reckoned that it was a good way to discover lanes that one never knew existed.

Pugsley's transport.

He remembers Snowdrop Valley when only a few people knew of it and recalls that the local folk, especially the women, became quite frightened when hordes of gypsies descended on the valley to pick the snowdrops. Sydney understood that the road past the valley known as Draper's Way was once the main route to Exford before the Exe Valley coach road was built. The old Exeter road from Minehead went up Bampton Street and over Grabbist Hill to Timberscombe. There the route went up beside the church and mounted the hill to the ridge along the Brendons which ran parallel with the new valley road below.

Many of the roads which were used at the time were little more than gravel tracks. Sydney wishes he could remember just when the bends on Porlock Hill were tarred. I wonder if any reader can remember? The road across to Selworthy Beacon did not exist as such until made up during the war by the army who used the area for manouevres and observation. Sydney believes that when the army left, joint maintenance was agreed between the National Trust and the Minehead Urban District Council. 'I always used to smile,' added Sydney, 'when I read M.U.D.C. The Mud Company. So inappropriate!'

Will Widden

Will Widden says…

Mr Sydney Whitehead's memories delighted readers. As someone said to me: 'He describes things that we can just remember which makes it particularly interesting and also stimulates our own memories.'

However I was surprised to receive a letter from a Mr Will Widden. At first I thought that it might be a joke, and then I wondered whether the letter would be written in incomprehensible dialect, but no! It was all straightforward. Will Widden really was the writer's name and why not for, as my correspondent pointed out, Widden is one of the oldest Devon family names.

Incidentally, just in case there are readers who don't remember Will Whidden, he was a wise old chap who passed on his pithy sayings to Jack Hurley who frequently ended his Notes by the Way column with 'Will Whidden says…' (Well, he was, wasn't he?!)

My Mr Widden's family came from Ilfracombe although he was born in Cardiff so they used to make great use of the White Funnel Steamers, owned by Messrs P. & A. Campbell, for journeys to and fro across the Bristol Channel. Will has always understood that he made his first trip to 'Combe in 1913 aged just three months.

'I can vouch,' he writes, 'for Mr Whitehead's reference to rough trips although my experience was that the crossing from Swansea to 'Combe could be even more exciting. We had many such trips but luckily all the family were good sailors.'

Will recalls one occasion when it was so rough that all passengers were ordered below. The *Cambria* was a very open ship, but his mother was very claustrophobic and could never go below so they were all allowed to remain on deck in view of the bridge.

One trip was particularly memorable. Will's family were on holiday in Ilfracombe when his father developed a mastoid. The local Cottage Hospital could not operate and, although the family had travelled to 'Combe the long way round by train, the doctor said that they must return immediately that afternoon by boat and he would telephone Cardiff Royal Infirmary as they would need to operate immediately on arrival.

The trip home was uneventful until after we left Minehead. Dad was in the saloon and Mother was on deck with me, a ten-year-old, as

PEOPLE

go-between. Just off Barry Roads we ran into a thick bank of fog and bumped a Greek steamer. Most passengers raced to the bows, Mother went under the bridge and Dad worried.' Eventually a pilot boat escorted them into Cardiff where an ambulance was waiting at Pier Head so everything tuned out all right in the end.

Will recalls that the steamers played an important part on many occasions during his life and not least when, in an indirect way, a journey by steamer led to him getting together with his wife to whom he was married for 57 years.

Looking in the *Free Press* at the advertisements for this summer's outings, Will couldn't help comparing fares. Minehead to Ilfracombe, returning by road, was £14.95. In his youth the day trip from Cardiff to Ilfracombe, returning by sea, cost 6s 6d; afternoon return, 4s 6d.

Will also remembers some of the old 'Campbells' cries'. Approaching the Foreland it was always 'Lower deck for Lynmouth!' while whatever the weather, the deck boy with the Fry's tray would be shouting, 'Choclits, sigrettes and pepsin' in a Bristol accent. At that time the boat bills were printed by Dates of Cardiff where the compositor in charge was Will's uncle.

Will included in his letter some information about the steamers and their eventual destinies which I have noted here together with other information that has come my way. I know I am always on dodgy ground when I write about ships because so many people are far more knowledgeable than I, but I also know that readers will soon tell me of any errors or send additional information!

The *Ravenswood*, was, I believe, the second ship to he operated by P. & A. Campbell in the Bristol Channel. She was launched in 1891 and eventually scrapped in 1955 after serving in two world wars. *Glen Usk* (1914) was used as a mine-sweeping flotilla leader during the two wars and was recommended as a model for future mine-sweepers. The *Glen Avon* (1912) foundered in a storm off the French coast while on naval service.

Westward Ho!, ordered in 1893, was at one time the most progressively-designed ship in the fleet. She was used as a Royal Naval accommodation ship at Dartmouth during the Second World War and did not return to P. and A. Campbell afterwards. Her sister ship, *Cambria*, also served as a Royal Naval accommodation ship, this time at Harwich and eventually ended her life as a hulk in the Thames Estuary. Both were scrapped in 1946.

The *Brighton Queen* was sunk while ferrying troops from Dunkirk and the *Brighton Belle* went down while returning to Dunkirk after landing in England. The *Devonia* was lost at the same time, being purposely beached to facilitate the embarkation of British soldiers. 'It was her last service, but perhaps the most useful, as she was the means of saving numbers of lives.'

Fred Partridge

The justified pride of Mrs Partridge

I received a most interesting letter from Mr Fred Partridge who lived at North Newton. Mr Partridge was born at Luccombe in 1911 and lived there for 25 years and his attention was caught by the account of a Selworthy cricket match in this column. He wondered whether the Petheridge who played cricket for Selworthy was actually a Petherbridge for he remembers Petherbridges in the area. During the First World War, it was a Mr Petherbridge who mended boots and shoes in the little thatched building between the school and the blacksmith's shop at Allerford. A Mrs Petherbridge kept a sweet shop just beyond the post office.

Early in the 1920s Mr Petherbridge retired to Minehead, possibly to the area around Cher. At that time Mr Partridge was a pupil at the private boys' school known as 'The Modern' which was situated in the red brick building at the back of Townsend House. Mr Petherbridge could often be seen walking briskly up or down Selbourne Place. He wore knickerbocker trousers and thick socks and liked to whistle loudly as he walked.

Mr Partridge was also wondering about the remains of the old chapel at Chapel Cross, the crossroads where the road over Dunkery meets the roads to Luccombe, Horner and Allerford. He recalled the foundations of the walls being more obvious than they are today and had a particular reason for remembering that area of grass at the highest point between Luccombe and Horner very well.

Just after the First World War, Mrs Floyde and her niece, Alice, opened what was to become the Horner Tea Gardens. Mr Partridge's mother supplied, in season, three pounds of clotted cream daily, and more if she had it. It was his job as a young boy to walk with the basket of cream to the highest point near Chapel Cross where Alice would meet him and there they would exchange pots, full for empty. He did not walk on down towards Horner because his 'little legs' would have had to walk back up the hill again before going to the village school.

Mrs Partridge was very proud of her venture and rightly so. Three pounds of cream at 2s 6d a pound seven days a week provided a good cash flow when adult farm workers were only receiving pay in the region of 28s to 32s a week. To celebrate her success Mrs Partridge took her small family for a special treat. They travelled from Minehead Pier to Watchet by paddle steamer to view the battle cruiser HMS *Fox*, which was anchored off Watchet prior to being brought into the harbour to be broken up by the Cardiff Marine Stores Company, a ship-breaking concern who had rented the West Pier for this purpose. At 7,000 tons, she was the largest ship ever to enter Watchet Harbour.

Very little is known about the old chapel which stood at Chapel Cross. While one school of thought thinks it may have been founded as a manorial chapel by Geoffrey of Luccombe in 1310, Charles Chadwyck-Healey *(A History of a Part of West Somerset 1901)* was certain that it was not. That chapel, he considered to be the one at Horner, dedicated to St Peter, that disappeared long ago. The chapel at Chapel Cross appears to have been dedicated to St Andrew. In February 1776 Mrs Wentworth granted a lease of 'Steer's Tenement, 2 acres near the chapel of St Andrew.' A Holnicote estate map of 1809-12 shows Steers Barton (two acres, one rod, eight perches) sited two fields away from the chapel.

Just why a chapel should have been founded here in this relatively remote spot on the road down from Dunkery is not clear. The other small chapels in this area, Tivington, Lynch, and the two at Blackford and Horner that have disappeared, were all sited near manor houses or at least small hamlets. Crossroads in pre-Reformation days were often marked by stone crosses and maybe this chapel grew up near the cross at an appropriate point for travellers to offer thanks for a safe journey over the moor.

When Prebendary Hancock led an excavation of the ruins of St Andrew's Chapel in the 1890s he was told by 'a very ancient person who happened to pass ... that her forebears had always known that a chest of gold lay buried beneath the building.' He was, however, not fortunate enough to secure this interesting treasure and only unearthed some old knives and a silver instrument, 'the use of which is uncertain.'

It is rumoured that the place is haunted but Mr Partridge didn't mention meeting any disturbed spirits on his trips to meet Alice.

However Mr Chadwyck-Healey reported that 'many people shudder now to pass the Chapel Cross at Luccombe at night. The spectre there is believed to be especially vindictive and chases the unhappy wayfarer in various forms, now a deer, now a boar and even sometimes a ram, so it is said.'

George Hosegood

Enthusiastic journal in fits and starts

There must be many people who, at the beginning of January, resolve to keep a daily journal and then find that, after an enthusiastic start, entries become shorter, whole days and even weeks are missed and eventually the whole enterprise grinds to a halt and is abandoned.

This is what happened with George Culverwell Hosegood who was farming at Escott Farm, Rodhuish, in 1849. His diary, lent to me by a descendant of his, begins on 1 February that year and is kept carefully until the end of April. Maybe pressures of work in May prevented him from keeping his journal for he takes up his pen again in June but by mid-July the whole thing has petered out. There are just a couple of late entries: the wedding of a friend, which took place on the same day as Williton Fair, and the marriage of his brother Obed, Obadiah, to Mary Ann Corner of Torweston, just before Christmas.

George was the son of Andrew Hosegood, the first of that family to be associated with Methodism in West Somerset. Farming at Capton, Andrew was influenced by his friend and neighbour, William Stoate, who farmed at Aller at Williton and who was the son of John and Mary Stoate. In 1786, John had left West Somerset for Bristol where he had set up business as a maltster and miller and had come under the influence of Methodist preachers and become an ardent convert. He returned to West Somerset in 1799 and the next year moved to Williton to a new house which he had built on the site of the present National Westminster Bank. There was no chapel, so services were held in this house until a building behind Fore Street became available.

In 1844, when William went to join his brother as a miller in Watchet, Andrew Hosegood took over Aller Farm. His brother James farmed at Bridge Farm, Williton. By 1849, George appears to have been managing Escott for his father with his sister Emma acting as his housekeeper. During March and April, he seems to have been making arrangements to take over the lease of Escott on his own account.

George was very close to his father, frequently visiting Aller and staying for the night.

Besides his brother Obed and sister Emma, George had a sister Ellen, who boarded at Mrs Stevens' school at Hainshill [Haines Hill] in Taunton. On one of his many trips to Bristol market, George broke his journey in order to visit Ellen and take her out into the town. Three younger sisters, Mary, Sarah Ann and Jane, were boarding in Dunster at a school run by Mrs Boyns. Quite often George or Emma would visit the children in Dunster and it seems to have been to Escott that they often came for holidays. George rarely mentions his mother, though once he records that he had breakfast with 'Father, Mother, Harry and James', the latter perhaps two younger brothers.

One thread running through the diary is that of George's growing faith and conversion. Nearly every Sunday he attended a place of worship, morning, afternoon and evening. Very often this was the chapel at Washford, built in 1824 and a vigorous and influential centre of local Methodism. Usually George recorded the name of the preacher as well as the text on which the sermon was based. His conversion may have taken place in February, for he writes: 'Evening I went home to father and slept there the night. From the good advice my father gave me I made a full determination to give my whole heart and soul to God and from this time I hope I may forever live nearer to the glory of God.'

It is interesting to note that George, as a Wesleyan Methodist, regarded himself as a member of the Church of England. On occasion, he attended Withycombe Church where he heard Mr Cook, the rector, preach and more often went to Rodhuish Chapel where Mr Tripp, the Vicar of Carhampton, would take the service. Many young men and women attended services throughout the day, sometimes lunching in one family's home, taking tea at another and often finishing up with supper and conversation at a third. George was a regular visitor to the Symons' home in Bilbrook where open house was kept after meetings at Washford. As a young bachelor, George seems to have been popular with the ladies and occasionally notes that he walked one of them home.

Two incidents remind us that George lived at a time when attitudes to wrong-doing were severe. On 26 March he wrote: 'Caught James Willis stealing eggs, turned him and his family away – his wife been confined a few days before, I cannot turn them out the house for a week or two.' He adds: 'Took Benjamin into the house as a servant.'

Was this another Willis child and an attempt by George to help'?

Not long after, on 7 April at about half-past-eight at night, he caught George Cooksley, of Golsoncott, stealing a deal plank from the saw pit. It took more than a fortnight for a warrant to be obtained, signed by John Halliday the magistrate, and delivered to the constable. On 4 July, Cooksley's case was heard at Bridgwater Quarter Sessions. He was sentenced to a month on the treadmill at Wilton Gaol.

Common turnips and drinking tea

Weather is of particular importance to farmers so it's not surprising that more often than not George Hosegood noted the day's weather in his diary. 1849 seems to have been typically unpredictable. February started mild and the men were able to get ahead with the work at Escott Farm, Rodhuish, but there was snow and boisterous wind by the end of the month. March went out like a lion while in April there were days of bitter cold with flurries of snow.

In spite of this, they were able to get ahead with the garden. Some peas and beans were sown early in February, on 24 March Robert began to sow the rest of the seeds and, by 27 March, all the vegetable seeds were in save for the French beans.

Most days George recorded the work being done on the farm though he rarely mentioned his labourers by name. Bullocks or oxen were still being used for ploughing and George's emotive phrase, 'Bullocks [or ploughs] crossing Marland', conjures up the slow plodding nature of this winter work. In Barnclose, sheep had been folded on to 'common' turnips during the winter months while swedes in another part of the field were lifted and stacked in Meadow. At the beginning of February, wheat was sown where the turnips had been and later the rest of the field was sown with barley. Horses were used for harrowing and other work. Towards the end of February, wheat was being threshed with the aid of 'Mathew's Machine' and Mr Giles, from Withycombe Farm, called up to see it working. Only a few years earlier, in other parts of the county, the introduction of these threshing machines, which did the work of several men, had been so unpopular that there had been riots and rick-burning.

That year, haymaking at Escott began on 3 June and, in spite of some stormy days, was completed within the month. Feeding the soil was a matter of considerable importance. On many days, horses were hauling dung and on one occasion hauled mud from the Lower Pond to the Waggon House to be mixed with guano. Later in the year, experiments were carried out with differently proportioned mixtures of ashes, earth, guano and lime.

The smithing work at Escott was contracted to Nathaniel Edbrooke for five years at an annual fee of ten guineas and when a bullock got a piece of turnip stuck in its throat George sent for the farrier, Robert Sully, who cupped and bled the animal before removing the turnip. Although some stock was disposed of locally, oxen at Williton Fair and pigs to local villagers, most went to Bristol Market. The Bristol and Exeter Railway, which linked Taunton and Bridgwater with Bristol, was completed by 1844 and farmers were soon using it to transport their animals. George would travel up to Bristol on the day before market day, setting off on horseback from Escott or his father's farm at Aller and usually catching the train at Bridgwater, although occasionally he went to Taunton to the bank and carried on from there. The sheep were driven to Bridgwater and pastured overnight on Pawlett marshes before being loaded into trucks for the journey to Bristol. There were occasional delays because of the number of animals being carried. Once they reached Bristol, the sheep were driven on to Mr Angers' land on the hill at Totterdown where some, destined for the butcher, were shorn. Cattle were sometimes sold as well.

George always put up at the Saracen's Head, White Lane, where he frequently ran into neighbours and acquaintances like Mr T. and Miss Ennor from Treborough who were heading for Liverpool and, perhaps, the New World. Sometimes George would go to chapel in the evening and later on enjoy a beefsteak or refreshments with friends. Once he met up with Mr Biffen of Charlengs [Charlynch] and they shared a room because the Inn was so busy.

In the morning, George would rise at 4.30am, fetch the sheep from Totterdown and have them penned and ready by 5.30am. Throughout the period of the diary trade was described as dull and prices were low. In the very first entry, George noted the 'Commencement of Free Trade' but any expectation that this would bring immediate benefits to the farmer were clearly not realised. The new ease of access to the market must also have helped to keep prices low, for George remarks on the numbers of sheep coming from Devonshire as well as Somerset.

It seems surprising, but one of the activities that George seems to have enjoyed most was 'drinking tea' in the afternoon. Wherever he was, enquiring about sheep, on his way back from market, buying seed corn, attending chapel or just being at home during a day's work on the farm, there is frequently a reference to drinking tea, often with a number of friends and relatives. We usually think of afternoon tea as a drawing room activity of the gentry, but it was obviously an important social occasion for the families of many of the working, but gentlemen, farmers of the area as well.

Sarah Biffin

Merry face masked hard life of indignities

I am sure that the story of Sarah Biffin will be familiar to many readers but some may not have heard it and others may like to be reminded. Sarah Biffin was born in East Quantoxhead in 1784 without hands or arms and with stunted legs. Her parents were ordinary poor labourers but they must have cared for Sarah devotedly for she grew to be a woman of independent thinking, lively, happy and intelligent. From a child she showed remarkable aptitude for drawing and painting using a pen or brush held in her mouth. She was also adept with needle, thread and scissors and became an accomplished needlewoman making her own clothes with careful, neat stitches.

Sarah's first lessons in art came from a Mr Dukes who soon suggested that Sarah should stay with him for a certain number of years and travel round exhibiting her talent at country fairs and circus sideshows. She was only 37 inches tall and was, in fact, viewed as a sideshow freak. Her act included signing her name, making small landscape drawings and, for an extra fee of three guineas, painting a miniature portrait of a customer.

People who saw her described how she would use a long-handled pen or brush scooping it off the table with her tongue and putting the end under a pin on the top of her right shoulder. She then used the pen or brush by moving it with her lips. When they were not in use, the pens and brushes were slipped into loops on the shoulder of her dress. Sarah was treated with kindness by Mr and Mrs Dukes but there was some indignation when it was discovered later that she had received an annual salary of only £5 in addition to her keep.

After a while, Sarah was befriended by the Earl of Morton who first suspected her of fraud and took his own portrait away with him each night until Sarah had finished it, so proving that it had not been painted by another artist. Lord Morton arranged for her to have watercolour lessons with the well-known miniaturist, William Marshall Craig, and also tried to get her release from the contract with the Dukes, but they refused all reasonable offers. Sarah could have repudiated it herself but kept honourably to the agreement which went on for 16 years.

For a while after that, Sarah was based in London and Lord Morton was able to introduce many wealthy patrons who, over time, included George III, George IV, William IV, Queen Victoria and Prince Albert. Sarah became quite a celebrity and was even mentioned in some of Charles Dickens' novels. In 1821, her miniatures were awarded a prize medal by the Society of Arts.

When she was 40, she contracted a mysterious marriage with a Mr Wright. It was an unhappy move; they never lived together and parted very soon. Rumours went round that Wright had married her with the intention of appropriating her money but Sarah denied these charges. 'On the contrary,' she said. 'When I married I had but £10 in all the world.' And indeed, for as long as he was able, her husband paid her £40 a year out of his own meagre income.

In about 1843, Sarah moved to Liverpool and only by working extremely hard and with the help of kindly patrons was she able to make a bare living for herself. By this time, the Earl of Morton had died and so she had no-one to help her obtain orders, sell her miniatures or introduce her to new patrons. She was reduced to writing to former patrons to ask if they were interested in purchasing her work.

Among her surviving letters is a sad note written in February 1850, the year she died. 'Miss Biffin begs to return her heartfelt thanks to Mr Matthew Gregson for the 10s so kindly sent to her. Miss Biffin would have written before but she has been very unwell. Is it towards the Fund or for her present use?' Her courage, courtesy and sense of honour were with her to the end.

As she grew older, she found it more and more difficult to summon up the energy needed to carry out her painting. Her eyesight began to fail and she was reduced to living in real poverty. Fortunately, one of her patrons, Richard Rathbone, heard of her plight and launched an appeal for subscriptions to purchase an annuity for her. Hundreds of erstwhile patrons were contacted and although the appeal did not reach its target of £1,000 it did raise £300 which provided Sarah with a small but regular income. Among subscribers were the actor

Macready and the Swedish nightingale, Jenny Lind. Subscribers from Somerset included the Revd John Poole of Enmore.

Sarah did not live to enjoy this income for long: she died three years later at the age of 67. Mr Rathbone gave Sarah's letters to the Liverpool Library and gave to the museum her self-portrait which shows a round-faced smiling woman, her deformity carefully hidden and a painting brush hooked to her shoulder. She wears a dark satin dress and lace cap and her merry expression gives little indication of the hard life and indignities that she had endured.

Betsy Bushen

The memories of Mrs Betsy Bushen

I own a copy of a photograph of a wonderful old lady, Mrs Betty or Betsy Bushen of Quay Street, Minehead, taken in her 101st year. At the foot of the photograph it reads: 'A great comfort to me has been Wiveliscombe Old Ale. I have had half a pint every night for 70 years; it gives me strength and sleep.' Mrs Bushen died later that year, 1909, on her 101st birthday. In 1901 Clement Kille recorded some of her childhood memories.

Elizabeth Bushen was born on Christmas Eve 1808 in London and was christened in Westminster Abbey. She was the daughter of a soldier named William Cooksley who was killed in Portugal during the Peninsula War when she was just six weeks old. Her mother had a sister living in Bossington so they left London to live with her. Until 1834, when she married a Minehead man, Betsy lived in the Selworthy area. She lived during the reigns of five monarchs and remembered the Battle of Waterloo, and the people of Bossington making an effigy of Bonaparte and burning it on Bossington Hill.

Betsy remembered the revels at Bossington where wrestling was the chief amusement. 'It was very severe,' she said,

Mrs Betsy Bushen of Quay Street, Minehead, in 1909 aged 100.

'and the men used to kick one another badly.' Bossington revels were held on Holy Thursday, when wrestling took place on the green. The revel, not the wrestling, was continued on Sunday. People came from Minehead, Watchet and other places by boat. Parson [Sylvanus] Brown of Porlock put a stop to the revels.

At Porlock the stocks were kept under a wide gateway at the entrance to the churchyard. Betsy once saw a man called William Pope in the stocks. At Selworthy the stocks were kept near the church. She remembered an old man named Ferris who lived at Buckethole who used to drive a bull in a putt like a horse. Ploughing was generally done with oxen. People used to cut the fern and burn it to make lye for washing clothes and this was sold to the gentry for a shilling a peck. There was no soda in those days.

Salt was needed for preserving and Betsy remembered carrying 11s to Captain Perkins of Porlock Weir for a quarter of a hundredweight (28lbs) of salt. When her mother killed the pig a quarter of it had to be sold in order to buy the salt. Wheat was a guinea a bushel, potatoes a £1 a bag; tea 10s to 12s a lb; loaf sugar 1s to 1s 2d a lb; moist sugar 8d to 9d a lb. A loaf cost a shilling and a bushel of coal, sixpence. Wages were 6s a week but house rent and the potato ground were cheap. There was no tea in those days for poor people who used to burn a crust of bread and put it in the tea-pot. They also used herb organ [sweet marjoram] and peppermint. They would eat a good deal of barley rather than wheaten bread.

Betsy remembered when William, eldest son of Farmer Clarke at East Lynch, was stolen by the gypsies. The late Mr J.K. Ridler also remembered being told this tale. Apparently at East Lynch there is – or was – a stone in the wall with the inscription, '1823. W.C.' These were the initials of William Clarke who was the brother of Mr Ridler's grandfather. 'My grandfather had trouble with gypsies who used to camp at the bottom of Great Headon. Sir Thomas Acland at Holnicote had had this land planted with trees and the gypsies would keep stocking his young grass with horses and one day, thinking he would teach them a lesson, he impounded the horses.

'The gypsies then turned spiteful and one day, soon after, a little boy, William Clarke, came up towards Headon to pick some rabbits' food and the gypsies took him and carried him away for some distance. A hue and cry was raised and everyone was out looking for the boy, so the gypsies abandoned him. The boy did not know where he was but suddenly he caught sight of a dealer who had been to East Lynch only a few days before and called out to him. The dealer took him home.' Betsy Bushen recalled that William was recovered the same day near Alcombe.

Every year the Minehead hobbyhorse went to Porlock and on one occasion 'they got drinky' and the Porlock men beat them and stole their hobby-horse and put it up on Porlock church steeple. The hobby-horse went to Porlock in the years after that but the men took better care of it.

Betsy's parents, presumably her mother married again, were working one day on the lime kiln on Bossington beach and she and other children were picking blackberries nearby, when, under the hedge, they saw lying a number of kegs, bound together with ropes. They had been told about pixies and thought that maybe pixies had put the kegs there, and they were afraid so ran away and told no-one about it. Betsy never saw any other hint of smuggling until she came to Minehead, and then she remembered what she had seen as a child at Bossington.

Memorials on the Moor

A stone in memory

I attended a simple ceremony to mark the siting of two discreet stones at the heart of Exmoor in memory of Malcolm MacEwen and Guy Somerset, those stalwart fighters for Exmoor. While sitting on the remarkably dry grass, listening while friends and family honoured these two men, I had time to reflect, and realised that I was taking part in a tradition of placing memorial stones on Exmoor that goes back a very long way.

Perhaps the earliest and best-known of Exmoor's memorial stones is the enigmatic Caratacus Stone on Winsford Hill whose inscription dates back to the equally enigmatic Dark Ages. The stone, standing near an ancient trackway leading into the Barle Valley, was probably a marker long before it was inscribed sometime during the seventh to ninth centuries. The stone was mentioned as 'Langeston' in medieval perambulations of Exmoor but the inscription was apparently not known until the end of the last century when a number of antiquaries encouraged by J. Lloyd Warden Page got together to work out just what it said. It reads CARATACI NEPOS, the kinsman of Caratacus, and presumably reflects the proud claim of the deceased to descent from the Caratacus who held out from South Wales against the Roman invasion of Britain until about AD50.

Other ancient memorial stones include the Cavudus stone near Lynton and the cross-decorated Culbone Hill stone but for many people it is the more recent stones that catch the eye and hold the interest. Several of these were set up on the moor within a few years of each other in the 1930s.

The Froude Hancock Stone stands beside the Dulverton-Molland road near Anstey Gate. Philip Froude Hancock was born in 1865 at Wiveliscombe and was the fifth son of William Hancock, brewer and banker. Philip became chairman of the brewery on the death of his father in 1896. He was a fine rugby player, played for the county and was capped for England on several occasions, sometimes captaining the side. He was a tall, well-built man – in a family photograph he appears to stand at least five inches above his brothers – keen on hunting, and was noted for riding very large horses of 17-18 hands. Although he would usually send his groom ahead to a meet with his horses, as a young man he always chose to ride home to Wiveliscombe after the hunt, sometimes arriving in the early hours of the morning.

Philip died in 1933 and was buried in Wiveliscombe churchyard. The seventeenth-century communion rails in front of the altar in the church there were presented by his widow in his memory. West Anstey Common was a place he loved and so his friends decided to place a boundary mark there to serve as a memorial to him. The thirteen-ton boulder was dedicated by the Bishop of Taunton and subscribed for by over 500 friends.

Right over on the other side of the moor near Chapman's Barrows stands the Negus Stone. Robin Negus was born in 1915 at Devonport and in 1924 the family moved to Exford where his father, Colonel R.E. Negus, was master of the Quarme Harriers. Later they moved to live at Oare Manor. Robin was a kind, gentle boy, liked by all who knew him. He loved animals and spent many hours riding over Exmoor. His favourite spot was Chapman's Barrows above Radworthy where he used to sit looking out over the moor. In the summer of 1932 he went to a school camp where he developed poliomyelitis. The infection proved fatal and he died, just 17 years old. Colonel Negus had the memorial stone set up on the spot that Robin loved so much. The inscription reads: In loving memory of Robert Richard Negus, 'Robin', who loved this place. Born 8th February 1915, Died 2nd August 1932.

A third stone put up round about the same time was the Fortescue stone which stands looking up the Barle valley at the side of the road between Kinsford Gate and Simonsbath. This stone stands in memory of Sir John William Fortescue who was born in 1859, the fifth son of the third Earl Fortescue. He was a studious boy and later went on to become a Scholar and Fellow of Trinity College, Cambridge. For a time he worked in the diplomatic service as private secretary to the Governors of first the Windward Islands, from 1880-2, and then New Zealand, from 1886-90. He then spent time working at the Public Record Office before becoming librarian at Windsor Castle, a post he held from 1905 to 1926. John Fortescue was a military historian of the first rank, writing in a vigorous, lucid and graphic style. His publications include his multi-volumed *History of the British Army* as well as the Exmoor-based *The Story of a Red Deer*.

John was a keen shot, a redoubtable walker and a knowledgeable naturalist and he often stayed at Simonsbath Lodge. When he died in France in 1933, his ashes were brought back to England and scattered on the county boundary at Five Barrows. The memorial cairn above Simonsbath was built by the family at the suggestion of his widow.

Some of the information for this Notes by the Way *came from Joan Gifford's article' Memorial Stones of Exmoor' in the* Exmoor Review 1969.

Parson Froude of Molland

A wild, hunting parson

Anyone passing Molland Church on one particular Friday evening might well have wondered whether they had been transported back a couple of centuries. The church windows glowed, the bells rang out and a veritable crowd of people, some in smocks, some in bonnets and shawls, made their way to the church door. Then, if they had paused a while to listen, they would have heard the sound of hymns and psalms being sung to the 'old tunes' – Lyngham, Diadem and the Evening Hymn. Evensong, early-nineteenth century style, was in full swing.

The village of Molland is situated nearly 700 feet up on the southern edge of Exmoor. Its name is derived from the Welsh moel meaning a bare hill, so 'the land by the bare hill'.

The church is a simple fifteenth- and sixteenth-century structure which replaced an earlier building. Only the Norman font and two medieval bells remain from that time. Fortunately the church escaped Victorian restoration and the interior is memorable, pure Georgian, with dark box pews, three-decker pulpit and a screen which bears just the faintest hint of the architectural style of Sir Christopher Wren. If you have not yet visited Molland church you have a treat in store.

The box pews, some with handy hat-pegs, are remarkably comfortable, the panelled sides keeping out the draughts. At the rear of the church the pews are raised for the singers and musicians who would have led the services 200 or so years ago. At one side, the seats are foreshortened to accommodate the village's apprentice and pauper children. Above the sounding board of the three-decker pulpit, a trumpeting angel symbolises the raising of the dead at the last trump. In fact, the pulpit is not really three-decker, the stalls for the priest and clerk being on the same level. There is a spacious pew for the squire and another for the parson's family.

The fine Georgian screen with its attractive wicket gate encloses the chancel completely. A solid tympanum fills the space above the screen, on which is painted the royal coat-of-arms and the Ten Commandments. Above the coat-of-arms, in pride of place, is inscribed: 1808 L. Mogridge – Church warden; Rowlands – Painter.

Molland was held with the neighbouring parish of Knowstone from 1279 to 1915. For a while, the Froude family were patrons of the living, which may explain why the infamous John Froude was ordained and then succeeded his father to the benefice in 1804, remaining there for 49 years. This 'unspeakable oaf' was the model for Parson Chowne in R. D. Blackmore's *The Maid of Sker* and so many stories have been linked with his name that it is hard now to distinguish fact from fiction.

John Froude was not merely a wild, hard-drinking, hunting parson. He was reputed to be a tyrant, feared for miles around by every man, woman and child. It was said that he had the Evil Eye and that he 'controlled a ruffianly tribe of young farmers and grooms who were always ripe for mischief and always at the parson's beck and call'. (A. Elliott-Cannon, *Exmoor Review* 1967).

At his instigation, they set fire to the ricks of farmers who had opposed him, got his curate too drunk to take Evensong and, on one occasion, prepared a boggy trap to ensnare the Bishop of Exeter when he came to remonstrate with the vicar.

Froude had been attacked in the press for neglecting his duties and the reforming Bishop Phillpotts had sent for him to give account of himself. There was certainly plenty to complain about. Months would pass without a service at Molland and then, suddenly, Froude would arrive unannounced. The congregation would arrive hurriedly 'to find the clerk stabling Froude's horse under the tower and the vicar donning a grubby surplice.' From the pulpit he thundered his way through the service, fixing his cowering parishioners with his hypnotic gaze, the sounding board making his voice reverberate around the church. Then he would depart as quickly as he had come.

Since Froude had made no attempt to go to see him, the Bishop decided to visit Knowstone. It was a cold day and he found the parson huddled over a fire, but every attempt to open discussion on serious matters was cut short by Froude's irrelevant replies. Then Froude began to press hot water and brandy on the bishop as a specific against the cold of the return journey. 'It's my only doctor, my lord, is a drop of brandy; and if I had but taken it when I got my chill, I shouldn't now be as I be, deaf as a haddock and nursing this ear like an old woman.'

Seeing that nothing was to be gained by continuing the interview, the bishop left. Ten minutes later, Froude was jogging off to a meet.

The Sayer Family of Dulverton

Person of sober life and conversation

When Tom Sayer died in 1929, he was the last of four generations of his family to serve Dulverton parish church as sexton and, in some cases, clerk. Born in 1845, he spent 14 years of his early life in Bath City police force, returning to Dulverton in 1879 to assist his ageing father with his responsibilities which included looking after the church clock and ringing the 'curfew' bell as well as grave-digging. As the years went on, Tom took over from his father and became a highly respected figure in the town and a fount of local knowledge. The year before his death, he was presented with an illuminated address marking his long and faithful service as sexton and verger.

Tom Sayer, his father, grandfather and great-grandfather before him, had notched up between them a total of 148 years' service to the church. The first Thomas Sayer was appointed clerk on 16 October, 1781 when, at a vestry meeting, it was resolved to dismiss Richard Pile from being clerk 'as we do think him highly improper for the said office in every respect.' Thomas Sayer, appointed in his place at an annual salary of £2 5s, was considered 'a proper person of sober life and conversation.' In 1795, Thomas also became sexton and grave-digger in place of John Graddon and in 1812 his salary as sexton was raised from £2 5s to £4 4s and as clerk to £3 3s.

In March 1817, following Thomas' death, his son John took over as sexton and possibly clerk as well. It was during John's term of office in 1831 that a burglar broke into the church and stole the communion plate, the Elizabethan chalice and paten dated 1573. The thief, John Baker Gould, was caught, convicted at the Taunton Assize and sentenced to seven years' transportation. He had tried to sell the pieces to a jeweller in Exeter who brought them back to Dulverton and was paid 15s 10d expenses for so doing.

In 1833, John Sayer took on the additional responsibilities of 'attending to the clock and chimes,' for which he was paid £1 a year, and ringing the morning and evening bell for which he received £1 7s. John died in February 1855 and I do wonder whether the drastic restoration of the church he had loved and served all his life helped to hasten his end. He did not live to see the new church consecrated.

The new parish clerk was John Daniel Prideaux but, although there is no minute of the appointment of Robert Sayer as sexton, he was certainly being paid in 1855 to clean the church, wind the clock and ring the morning and evening bell. By 1848, Robert Sayer had been appointed organist in place of George Graddon who had held that position for 50 years. Robert may well have deputised for the old man before 1847 for an item in an old sexton's notebook reads proudly: 'The Lord Bishop of Bath and Wells held his confirmation here at Dulverton and about 130 were confirmed. He came from Dunster and leaved here for Wiveliscombe. I, Robert Sayer, played the organ at his coming in church. There was only the Litany read and after the sentence after the laying on of hands I had to play the Amens instead of the clerk.'

Robert Sayer died in March 1894. He was considered a musician of extraordinary talent, able to play most wind and string instruments and in much demand at dances and parties, both as a fiddler and as a singer of 'quaint old-fashioned comic songs.' Tom Sayer was his son.

In 1873, during Robert's time as sexton, a scandalous epitaph on a gravestone was placed in the churchyard at Dulverton. It read:

Neglected by his doctor
Treated cruel by his nurse

His brother robbed his widow
Which makes it all the worse.

It is not surprising that the vicar demanded the epitaph be removed and, when the widow responsible refused, he took the matter to the consistory court in Exeter. The lady still refused to give in and was sent to prison for contempt of court before eventually capitulating.

In 1908, the vicar of Dulverton decided to introduce antiphonal singing. In future, the verses of the psalms would be sung alternately, first by one side of the choir and then by the other. But the choir was not having this and all but one of the adult choristers went on strike. These verses were published in the London *Globe*:

Gone are his fellow songsters all
He stands alone, unheeding
The nimble choir that ran like hares
(The youthful trebles leading)
Because the vicar had a strong
Desire for antiphonic song.

How swift the mellow tenors ran
While weighty basses sprinted.
The vicar sighed, but brightened up,
 For one had not deserted.
Yes, one remained who saw no wrong
In singing antiphonic song.

And what a guerdon his will be
If only he can stick it;
For when the choir's beanfeast comes
Alone he'll take a ticket,
And eat the buns that don't belong
To foes of antiphonic song.

It's impossible to imagine Tom Sayer being party to such an affair!

Squire Nicholas Snow

Tales from Oare – or Ore or Ar

The name Oare – be it spelt Ar, Ore, or Ora as it was in medieval documents – comes from the Old English word *ora* meaning a bound or limit or edge. Just which bound it refers to is debatable for Oare marks the ancient limit of the County of Somerset, the boundary of the Hundred of Carhampton and was also close to the borders of the Royal Forest of Exmoor. Perhaps it even marked an earlier division between the lands of one Celtic tribe and the next.

Be that as it may, by the time of *Domesday Book* (1086) Oare was held by Ralph of Pomeroy. Edric had held it before 1066 and paid tax for one hide. There was enough arable land for six ploughs to work besides meadow, woodland and pasture and there were seven villeins and five smallholders as well as four slaves to work the lord's land. Multiply each by, say, five, and you get a population of about 80 – roughly the same as it was in 1800 and 1901.

Being close to the borders of the Forest, Oare was a good centre for poaching and for illegally cutting peat, removing saplings and taking timber. Records abound with incidents like that in 1270 when Walter of Ar and Adam le Bonde of Ar provided pledges for Matthew, the parson, who was fined 20 shillings for harbouring his son, Walter the Clerk, and his servant, John Elyot, who had brought home a hind that they had found shot by John Scrutenger of Cludesham. A likely tale!

Although remote, the scattered parish of Oare was organised in the same way as any other. A series of officials headed by the churchwardens and the overseers of the poor looked after the affairs of the parish, keeping the roads in order and caring for the sick. The earliest church record seems to be a volume entitled *Poor Book*, a precursor of the churchwardens' accounts which start in 1792. The accounts in the *Poor Book* run from 1734, when money was paid out to repair the bridge at Malmsmead (1s), for the use of the stocks (3s), and for making three journeys to appear before the justices (3s). Incidentally the cost of the new account book was 5s.

There may have been only a small population but the poor and the sick still needed care. In an article in the *Exmoor Review* (volume 6) the late Revd J.G. Brunskill singles out the case of James Motile who is supplied with a coverlette for his bed (1s 6d), and later two blankets, surprisingly expensive, 5s 6d. He was supplied with leather and nails

(1s) presumably to cobble up his boots but not long after was presented with a new pair of shoes. The overseers thought that ordinary parish relief was not sufficient: he was given 3s for extras 'in his distress above pay' and later the same sum was paid as 'more as a gift for him'. James' illness evidently became worse. Richard Berry, perhaps the surgeon, was paid for attending Moule but sadly and inevitably there follow payments for the coffin, the washing and stretching of the body, for making his grave, and for his affidavit Clearly the parish officers went about their business with thoroughness and compassion. The year's expenses had been great. Eight rates had raised £7 14s 7d but total expenditure was £8 1s 7½d so a special rate was levied to balance the books.

It was said that the Snow family had owned land in Oare since the time of Alfred but it was in the early 1700s that part of the manor, formerly owned by the Spurriers, passed to Nicholas Snow, whose son, another Nicholas, purchased the remainder in 1788 so becoming lord of the manor. It was, I believe, his great-nephew who was the model for 'Farmer Snowe' in *Lorna Doone*, a portrayal that angered the last, and perhaps greatest, Nicholas Snow.

George Barwick at Southernwood worked for this Nicholas Snow at Oare Manor for many years and remembered R.D. Blackmore coming there in about 1882. By then *Lorna Doone* had become popular and no doubt copies of the book had reached Oare. Mr Snow sent to Parracombe for Blackmore to come to see him and fixed day and time. George was doing jobs in the yard at about 11am when Mr Snow strolled out with his hat set well back, which meant, George said, that "zummit was brewing".

Presently Blackmore drove up and, on approaching the squire, touched the brim of his hat and no more. Without ado Mr Snow began. He considered it a great impertinence on the writer's part to have written about the Snows in the way he had. Blackmore expressed regret that

Oare Manor.

anything should have caused pain or ill-feeling; Mr Snow warned him never to write anything again about his family, and went into the house while the novelist left the yard. A short, sharp and memorable interview.

It is said that 'a little loving cup' was presented to Snow by Blackmore after this interview in reparation for his not wholly complimentary treatment of the family and that when the Prince of Wales was entertained to tea in August 1879 at Oare Manor he drank from the cup. But Edward MacDermot, the author of *The Royal Forest of Exmoor*, who knew Mr Snow, asserted that the story was 'false for he was sure Snow would never have accepted any present from Blackmore whom he disliked and called a darned liar.'

A Nimrod in the chase

In these years around the turn of the millennium I become more and more aware of how things have altered – not so much over the last thousand years, though of course they have – but in this last century: the motor car, the aeroplane, the devastation of two world wars, the phoenix-like rising of people again and again and again from the ashes, shopping, computers and so on. There have also been great changes in people's attitudes to all sorts of matters, and when I read the obituary notice for Nicholas Snow, lord of the manor of Oare, who died in 1914 aged 86, I realised that it was written in quite another world.

Squire Nicholas Snow was a man both loved and respected by all who knew him. 'His death has removed,' wrote his obituarist, 'one of the last, if not the last, of that one-time typical class of country gentlemen who farmed their own land, were simple in habits, though well-to-do, and who, above all, were Nimrods in the chase and loved field sports above all else in the way of recreation.'

For many years Mr Snow kept a pack of foxhounds known as 'The Stars of the West', later to become the Exmoor Foxhounds. An anonymous correspondent to the *West Somerset Free Press* wrote: 'I first knew [Mr Snow] in Jubilee year. In that year he celebrated the good Victoria's 50th year as a Sovereign in a unique way. Probably no Master of Foxhounds before and certainly no Master since ever had a meet of hounds in June. Those who have copies of the *Free Press* for that year and are curious, will find the following notice in the one dated June 18th, 1887, if they care to turn it up.

"The Exmoor Foxhounds will have a Jubilee Hunt on Tuesday, the 21st. Meet at Oareford at 5am."… A Jubilee jollity.'

I like the idea that people kept their copies of the *Free Press* for 25 years! I wonder whether they had them bound and if so, whether there are any bound volumes still around in old country house libraries.

Nicholas Snow did his duty as a JP, Poor Law Guardian and churchwarden, and was regarded as the most generous and courteous of men. Dr Francis Hayes of Dunster, writing in 1925, described him as the King of Oare who dispensed hospitality in a princely manner. 'When I think of what he did in this line for a very long period of years and of the crowds that availed themselves of his cordial invitations, it is little wonder he died a poor man.'

The housekeeper at Oare Manor was Maria, 'the greatest curer of hams of all time', both in number and super-excellent quality, while her home-made bread and raspberry jelly were memorable.

Though so kindly, Nicholas Snow was, said Dr Hayes, an autocrat and objected to any infringement of his rights. In order to keep his right-of-way over a wooden bridge that he had built for the use of the public crossing Badgworthy Water, he was accustomed, on a certain day each year, to charge a toll of one penny. On one occasion, a man pushed past Steere, his keeper, refusing to pay. Squire Nicholas had the bridge removed.

An interesting story is recorded in H.J. Marshall's book, *Exmoor – Sporting and Otherwise*. (1948) 'When as a young man, Mr Snow inherited the manor, he came across a number of old books dealing with witchcraft and the black arts. Some ancestor had evidently dabbled in those matters and left these books behind him.

'Nicholas Snow at once burnt the books and confided the matter to his neighbour Squire Halliday. But local belief in witchcraft could not be disposed of as easily as that. In the lane below the Manor, a holly tree once stood. Underneath it was a gate. Local legend connected this spot with a witch known locally as Molly, who had lived there some 100 years ago. Few dwellers in the valley were courageous enough to pass that spot after dusk. It was believed that Molly sometimes appeared there, a diminutive figure some six inches high standing on the gate, or as a white hare in the lane.

Another story is that of the ghostly parson who appears when a new parson is inducted to the living of Oare. On the evening when Mr Marshall's brother was inducted to Oare, so the story goes, he was sitting in his study when he heard the sound of the church bell ringing. Wondering why, he started to walk up to the church in the twilight. On the way an old clergyman met him and passed by in silence, looking at him and smiling.

Attaching no importance to the incident, he went on to the church and found everything in order and the door shut. Later he mentioned the incident to an old parishioner and was then informed, to his amazement, that when a new rector was inducted at Oare a certain predecessor was wont to come back and ring him in.

Believe it or not!

Gates on the Moor, Alfred Vowles and the Comer Family

Landmarks of Utility

These days there are very few gated roads left on Exmoor so it may come as a surprise to realise that earlier in the twentieth century there were nearly fifty gates crossing Exmoor's roads. These were real gates that needed to be opened and shut as the traveller passed through if stock was to be kept grazing where it should. Writing in February 1949, Alfred Vowles noted that many of the gates on Exmoor had, by then, become damaged or had disappeared completely. Yet more and more animals were being grazed and the slow but steady growth in motor traffic made the need to keep stock off the roads more urgent.

Vowles described the gates as being 'landmarks of utility; their names beautifully descriptive and household words to most of us; for generations many have been favourite meeting places for hounds hunting stag, fox and hare and for many other popular occasions. If they could speak as well as creak, drag, slam or bang what pretty stories of the highways and moors they could tell us.'

Of the fifty gates that once stood sentinel on the moor, Vowles reckoned that at the time he was writing nine had disappeared completely. These included County, Brendon Two, Black Pits, Driver Cott, Pinkery, Blue, South Hill (Winsford Hill end) Comer's and the one in Withypool Village south of the bridge. Of more than twelve still in situ but rarely closed were Scob Hill, Goat Hill, Mounsey Hill, Muddy Lane, Sweetworthy and Cloutsham. And of the twenty or so still in use Vowles named Lower Willingford Bridge, Molland Moor, South Hill (cottages), Harberry's, Halse Lane, Greystone and Dunkery Hill.

I have a correspondent who often takes me to task for not explaining exactly where places are. I have to admit that there are one or two names here with which I am not wholly familiar but I have a feeling that if I put some of the gates in the wrong places readers will soon put me straight!

County Gate on the Porlock – Lynton road is probably the most familiar of these points even today. On the Somerset – Devon border, the site in the thirteenth century was in the extreme north-west corner of Exmoor Forest where the perambulations of the Forest started or finished. In the records of the time it was variously written as Corseneshet, Corsnestake and Cornesyete while in 1300 it was Cornesgate. Later it was known as Cosgate and was perhaps associated with the Coscombe mentioned in a hunting report written by Charles Palk Collyns in 1813 in which the stag is said to have run 'to Coscombe now Glenthorne'.

E.T. MacDermot writing of Cosgate in his *History of the Forest of Exmoor* mentions that 'this place or the adjoining hill was called Cosgate long before the fence and gate were set up about 1840.' Vowles wondered whether County Gate was ever the toll gate and whether the keeper occupied the one-storeyed house nearby. By 1949 the old gate had long disappeared but the two big stone posts remained as reminders of it. It was of course a similar gatepost that had to be removed at Ashton Gate for the lifeboat *Louisa* to be taken through in 1898.

The gates at Brendon Two Gates, one of the best known landmarks on the moor, finally disappeared during the 1940s, as did Black Pits Gate a mile to the south, when the Exe Valley – Brendon Two Gates road was widened. These gates had been set up on the Brendon – Simonsbath road when John Knight built the wall to enclose the Forest in about 1829; this stretch also dividing Somerset from Devon and the Royal Forest from Brendon Common.

Originally two gates were hung here without fastenings, one on either side of the hanging post, which allowed travellers to pass through easily and ensured that one gate was kept closed whichever way the wind was blowing.

The story goes that before the remaining gate disappeared, gypsies began camping on Brendon Common for the sole purpose of closing the gate against motorists and opening after money had been handed over.

'Their frequent impudent demands and the free fight between two rival camps for the "right" to oblige motorists in this way appear to have brought matters to a climax for special legislation was passed to make camping on Brendon Common illegal and the Romanies vanished as did their companions at Scob Hill Gate one mile to the north.'

Brendon Two Gates. This photograph must have been taken before Alfred Vowles made his survey of Exmoor gates.

Between Simonsbath and Challacombe there were three gates, Goat Hill, Pinkery and Driver Cott, but Vowles seemed to think that only Goat Hill Gate was in use in the years prior to 1949 and then only occasionally. However Stan Curtis of Simonsbath remembered that in the 1930s the gate at Driver Cott was in full working order and generally kept closed. As a boy he earned a few welcome pence opening for motoring visitors.

A little fright at Blue Gate

After reading my *Notes* on Exmoor gates Julian Bruford kindly sent me a list of moorland gates on Exmoor with grid references. I was delighted to receive it and the list, together with Noel Allen's *Exmoor Place-names*, means that I can now identify the position of most gates, however long gone. To help the reader identify the sites as well, I include a four figure reference after the name of each gate.

Comer's Gate (8535) at the western end of Winsford Hill seems to have been mentioned first in a staghunting report of 1866. Alfred Vowles, in his 1942 article on the moorland gates of Exmoor, speculated that the first gate there might have been set up by a member of the Comer family. Winsford Hill was, and is, part of the Holnicote estate belonging then to the Aclands and now to the National Trust. During the middle of the last century the local estate carpenter was William Comer who lived at Cot, Bridgetown. Perhaps he built the first gate or maybe, as Noel Allen suggests, it was put up by John Comer who in 1840 was also an employee of Sir Thomas Dyke Acland.

Vowles noted that although the gate and side rails had been removed some years before 1942, the tradition of June pixies playing hide and seek in and out of the foxgloves close to the gate was still remembered.

Muddy Lane Gate (7932), or simply Mud Gate, was on the Withypool – Sandyway road where the Exmoor Forest boundary ran with the boundaries of the parishes of Hawkridge and Exmoor, the name being indicative of the state of the road in earlier times. At the time of writing a new gate was in position accompanied by instructions to 'close the gate'. Vowles thought it unlikely that hurrying motorists would respond to the appeal. 'Perhaps many of them,' he wrote, 'are in too much of a hurry to catch a view of the Cork and Bottle, a ruin a short way along the road towards the Sportsman's Inn.'

Roger Burton, in his book *Heritage of Exmoor*, suggests that the Cork and Bottle was not a real public house but simply a cottage farmhouse where ale was sold; perhaps the house at nearby Greenbarrow which was let down in the 1920s.

Blue Gate (7537) is still marked on modern OS maps. The gate was positioned where the Forest Boundary crossed the Simonsbath to North Molton road described by John Leland in 1540 as a 'high morisch hylle'. The area is perhaps better known to lovers of Exmoor's history as the site of one of the mines sunk for Frederic Knight in the 1850s. Why it should be Blue is not clear.

Vowles tells a story of how he once experienced 'a little fright' at this isolated spot some 1500 feet above sea level. Motoring towards Simonsbath one dark and foggy night he caught a momentary glimpse in the confused light of the headlamps of a grey blurred figure on the near side of the road. Thinking it was someone walking down to Simonsbath he pulled up and called out to see whether they would like a lift. A gale was blowing and he could hear no reply although he could still see the figure, 'dark and faintly silhouetted against the weak reflected light of the lamps and enveloped in driving mist which poured into the car through the near side window which had been let down.'

Getting no response and thinking that something must be wrong,

Vowles decided to investigate. He jumped out of the car and, as he stretched out a hand towards the figure, his fingers contacted a cold, hard, wet object. Not a human hand but a roadside post! Later he realised that this was the one remaining relic of the Blue Gate, eventually dug up and carted away.

Greystone Gate (8433) stood at the south-east corner of Withypool Hill on the road to Hawkridge. Vowles suggested that the gate took its name from a stone that once stood on this spot marking the boundary of the parishes of Winsford and Withypool which crosses Worth Lane at this point. Older maps mark this spot with BS – boundary stone.

It is perhaps worth remarking here that most of the gates crossed roads where boundaries of one sort or another met, so that stock grazing on common land could he kept within parochial or Forest bounds. Greystone Enclosures were first mentioned by Collyns in 1798 but the gate itself not until 1819.

Some gates have unusual names. Twizzlemark Gate (7141) stood near the Twizzell Markstone on the Challacombe – Exmoor Forest boundary. Noel Allen explains in his book that in West Somerset dialect, 'twizzle' is the top of a tree-trunk where the boughs branch out.

Hunger Gate (6939) on the county boundary between Challacombe and Brayford was probably a name of reproach for an area where nothing much would grow while Louisa Gate (9328) was a poshed-up version of Lousy Gate. Lousy is dialect for pigsty and from the Gate, situated above Barlynch Woods between Heath Poult and Dulverton, the road leads down to Swine Cleave.

No frequenting of taverns or ale houses

In a letter received soon after Landmarks of Utility *was published Mrs Gillard of Bradninch explains that she is descended from the Comers of Winsford and is able to explain exactly how Comer's Gate got its name.*

She writes: 'Several generations of my family were employed on the Acland estates, both at Holnicote and at Killerton. Sir Thomas was at one time in dispute with the Fortescue Estate concerning land adjoining Winsford Hill, and John Comer, well respected by both parties was called to give evidence in Court.'

Mrs Gillard has the reference given to John Comer to produce in Court and kindly sent me a copy. It is dated 5 February 1852 and reads: 'We the undersigned hereby certify that we have known John Comer of the Parish of Winsford many years and have every reason to believe him to be a well-disposed and honest character. He himself and his wife are regular in their attendance at Church and altogether quiet and respectable persons.' The document was signed by Bennett Michell, the vicar of Winsford; Joseph Relph, the rector of Exford, and George Clatworthy, churchwarden at Winsford.

Incidentally it is interesting to recall that the Revd Bennett Michell, vicar of Winsford from 1824 to 1857, was the father of Ellen who married William Young and went to live in Crowcombe. Her family's wonderful photograph album featured in one of the first Notes by the Way that I ever wrote. Bennett Michell was also father of the Revd William Philip Michell who was Vicar of Carhampton during the latter part of the nineteenth century. The Revd Joseph Relph was the reforming rector of Exford who originated from Cumberland and kept his northern accent and country ways to the end.

To return to the story. In the event, with the respected John Comer speaking in Sir Thomas's favour, the matter was settled out of court and, in gratitude, Sir Thomas named the piece of disputed land after him. Hence Comer's Cross and Comer's Gate.

Some of the family later moved to Killerton to work and in 1871 Mrs Gillard's grandfather, also John Comer, was apprenticed to Broadclyst wheelwright, John Ayshford. In his indentures, signed on

Exmoor ponies at Comer's Gate. Alfred Vowles captions the card: 'What Exmoor ponies look like.'

2 March in that year, young John was bound apprentice to Ayshford until he reached the age of 21 'to faithfully serve him, his secrets keep, his commands honest and lawful shall and will obey.' He also promised not to be absent without leave, nor play at any unlawful sports or games, nor frequent taverns or alehouses, nor associate with profligate or evil-disposed persons, nor waste, embezzle or consume the goods, money or effects of his master. In all things he was to demean and behave himself as an honest, sober and diligent industrious and faithful apprentice.

In return for this devoted service his master would, to the best of his power, teach and instruct him, or cause him to be taught and instructed, in the trade and business of a wheelwright. John would receive no wages during the first year of his apprenticeship and then he was to be paid a shilling a week during the second year, two shillings during the third and so on. Hours of work were from six in the morning until seven in the evening with two hours allowed for meals. If John were to be ill for more than seven consecutive days his wages would be stopped.

And, for this, John Comer's father agreed to provide for his son, 'good and sufficient board, lodging and wearing apparel of all sorts fit for one of his condition or degree.' He would also provide medicine and medical attention in case of sickness and find all the requisite tools for the job needed for his son's term of apprenticeship, probably seven years.

Young John Comer must have given satisfaction for on 17 June 1882, John Ayshford wrote him a reference. 'I hereby certify that John Comer duly served his time with me has (sic) an apprentice in an honest and upright manner and worked for me years after.' John Comer later became Estate Foreman at Killerton.

Mrs Gillard's late father was also an apprentice at Killerton, later moving to Winsford in 1908 to live with his cousins, the Bevin family, and working for Mr James Steer until the beginning of the First World War.

5 HAPPENINGS

The Bread Riots

The hungry people grow insolent

On Sunday 7 September 1800, Parson Holland, of Over Stowey, observed three men deep in conversation on the stocks by the churchyard wall and wrote in his diary: 'I suppose the subject is the rise in provisions. I think it is a shame after so good a harvest that [the price of] corn should be so high. I shall thresh out a few bushells and divide it into pecks at a low price.'

For those who were hungry and desperate in our villages at the turn of the eighteenth century, any action which might lead to cheaper food had to be considered. While the farmers were blamed for the high prices and threatened with having their ricks burnt, it was to the overseers and the magistrates or Justices of the Peace that the people turned for help. While the overseers might be able to provide immediate assistance, it was the magistrates, local gentry like Sir John Acland at Fairfield and Mr John Evered at Hill, who had responsibility for both criminal and civil matters, including the pricing of goods and who were thought to have the power to direct the farmers to lower their prices.

Earlier, during the autumn of 1794, the labourers at Stogursey were already desperate. They appear to have been remarkably restrained in the action they took, simply pinning a note on a gatepost in the village threatening an armed uprising unless agricultural wages were raised. In May the following year, another note was pinned on the church door at Stogursey alleging that desperately needed wheat was being exported, and again threatening violence.

In 1795 a small demonstration took place at Nether Stowey. It was watched by young Morley Chubb, at boarding school in Nether Stowey, who wrote in a letter home: 'There was a small mob here on Monday when Sir Philip Hales came to have the corn carried away but there was no great damage done; we were none of us suffered to go out of the house.'

Five years later things were no better. In February 1800, the labourers at Stogursey compiled yet another note, this time complaining of starvation wages in the area, and this was pushed under the door of the Market House. In October that year Parson Holland commented on the rising tide of discontent in the area: 'The Overseers are harassed to death ... our poor rates are four times the sum they were two years ago. The Justices attend to every complaint and every scoundrel in the parish crowd to make their complaints.' The parson felt that the Justices needed to be more cautious and wary of granting all the demands of the people in hopes of keeping them quiet. The people 'grow insolent and subordination is lost ... I wish I could prevail upon the farmers to sell their wheat to the Parish at ten shillings a bushel and then keep the poor to their usual standard of allowance.'

Then on 31 March, 1801, a hundred labourers gathered together in Stogursey and set off with a petition intending to gather supporters from other villages and persuade the local magistrates to sign the petition in the hope that this would make farmers lower their prices. The petition demanded that prices should be reduced: wheat to be ten shillings a bushel; barley six shillings; peas six shillings; butter and bacon eightpence a pound and potatoes five shillings for a three bushel bag. When the demonstrators reached Nether Stowey they read out their grievances in the Market Place [the market cross then stood at the junction of Lime Street and Castle Street] and were joined by another hundred men. From there they marched over the hill to Goathurst where they hoped to find Major Tynte and Mr Parsons, local magistrates, but discovered that they had left for North Petherton in order to deal with a similar affair. The marchers, now numbering several hundred, set off for North Petherton but, when they got there, they found that the meeting had ended and the magistrates gone on to Taunton. By this time the demonstrators numbered a thousand.

They decided to march on to Bridgwater and here the military was called out. The marchers, all still behaving in an orderly manner, met with Mr Wollen who tried to confiscate the petition and inevitably a scuffle ensued. Mr Wollen lost his temper, gave Symons, a mason, a black eye and had his coat ripped down the back for his pains. Eventually matters quietened down, the marchers retrieved their petition and moved on through Wembdon and Cannington to Hill House at Otterhampton where Mr John Evered met representatives of the marchers. He wasn't prepared to sign the petition, but promised to do his best to see that food was made available to the men and their families at the lowest prices. Trusting in Mr Evered's integrity, the marchers dispersed.

The next day, 1 April 1801, Mr Evered met with four other magistrates at Bridgwater and together they issued a document calling for farmers to sell their corn at a price that will enable the Baker to afford the quartern, 4lb, loaf at tenpence. This was the price paid for bread by those men who attacked the bakery at Old Cleeve a few days later and who were hanged for their 'crime'.

The price of bread

On 15 April 1801 nine men were hanged at Stonegallows just outside Taunton. Two of them, William Tout, born at Wiveliscombe, and Robert Westcott, born at Withycombe, were hanged for stealing bread. They were charged with being part of a riotous assembly and breaking and entering the bakery of Richard Griffey at Old Cleeve on 30 March and putting into bodily fear and danger of her life, Mrs Mary Griffey. They were accused of forcing the door of the bakery and forcibly taking fifteen loaves of bread, worth 1s 6d each, and disposing of them.

Both agreed that they had had the loaves in their hands but Tout denied ever handling the pickaxe used to break down the door while Westcott claimed that they had paid 10d for each of the loaves, a price they considered reasonable.

Around the turn of the eighteenth century farm labourers in Somerset were living at near starvation levels and conditions had become so bad that some decided to take matters into their own hands in an attempt to bring down the price of basic foods. In March 1801, rumblings of discontent culminated in a full scale march and demonstration in villages near Bridgwater. The problem lay in low wages and the high cost of bread. The underlying cause was the huge rise in population during the eighteenth century. With so many mouths to feed there was soon just not enough food to go round and the pressures of supply and demand forced up the price of basics such as wheat.

By 1773 there was no wheat to spare for foreign markets and after 1800 Britain was compelled to buy in corn. The problem was aggravated from 1793 when the blockade of Britain during the Napoleonic Wars prevented the importation of foreign grain and led to the sinking of ships carrying cargoes of food.

The person most at risk was the agricultural labourer. Among the typical parishes surveyed in 1795 was Stogursey where families with up to five children were attempting to live on just over eight shillings a week. Poor people like Matthew Grose of Dodington died of hunger and were buried 'on the parish'.

In a petition prepared by the demonstrators it was stated that in 1801 a man's average wage was 1s 2d a day while the price of a quartern loaf (which could easily be eaten by one man in a day) was 1s 1d. With wages so low the labourer and his family had to turn to the parish for support and overseers' accounts for many Somerset parishes show huge increases in payments resulting in corresponding increases in the poor rate, paid by the householders of the parish.

The conditions were so bad by 1800 that in some places overseers were buying in food and selling it to the poor at less than cost. Sometimes the overseers supplemented the men's wages and so took away any incentive for the farmer to raise wages himself. Sometimes there was no money to help.

William Wordsworth, living at Alfoxden in 1797, was aware of what was going on. He wrote in his poem, *The Last of the Flock*:

> Six children, Sir, I had to feed;
> Hard labour in a time of need!
> My pride was tamed, and in our grief
> I of the parish asked relief.

Refused help, the poor smallholder gradually sold off his sheep to buy food.

> As fine a flock as ever grazed!
> Upon the Quantock hills they fed.

The Somerset farmer of the period gets a very bad press. William Jenkin, the Duke of Buckingham's agent at Dodington copper mines near Nether Stowey, placed the 'enormous advanced price of the necessaries of life' largely at the door of 'the unfeeling, Inhuman and Rapacious dispositions of your overgrown farmers, whose hearts I have often thought are too callous to admit of the least sense of feeling for the suffering of the starving poor around them.'

It was against this background that the incident at Old Cleeve took place. The judge at the trial said that those accused had paid 'their own price' for the loaves which was tantamount to taking the bread without paying for it at all. The men were found guilty and the judge in passing sentence, observed that they had been convicted upon 'a full and satisfactory evidence, of an offence of such magnitude that their lives were justly forfeited to the injured laws of their country. They had formed part of one of those mobs who, under the pretence of lowering the price of provisions, committed depredations on the community. It was therefore necessary that such offences should receive from justice the utmost punishment that the law could inflict.'

An eye witness at the execution at Stonegallows described the scene. 'It was about the time of the bread riots. The nine poor fellows were driven from prison to Bishop's Hull sitting on their coffins. The nine ropes for hanging were suspended from an erected gallows. As the ropes were placed around the necks of the men, the cart was drawn away from under them and they were left suspended. The nine men were hanged at once.'

Because there was fear of rioting mounted dragoons accompanied the men from Wilton gaol to the gallows but the event passed off quietly.

Traffic Concerns

Striking resemblance to a hay elevator

These days there is a great deal of concern over the ever-increasing volume of traffic on our roads. Each year the number of vehicles on Somerset's main roads seems to increase. Traffic through towns and villages causes hold-ups and does real damage to buildings while a constant stream of cars on country roads detracts from the peace and quiet of our rural areas. Turning the situation around will need a change of attitude and even an element of sacrifice from those of us who drive but it may be a comfort, albeit a very small one, to know that the residents of West Somerset were concerned about the traffic in 1908!

In that year nearly one hundred inhabitants of Minehead and the surrounding area signed a petition to prohibit a motor coach! It was addressed to Somerset County Council, Williton Rural District Council and Minehead Urban District Council and read as follows:

We the undersigned Owners and Occupiers of property in Minehead and its surrounding district, and who pay rates and taxes in respect of such property, humbly petition your various councils for our protection, to use your influence and powers to restrict, and if possible prohibit, the use in our District of a certain Motor Coach owned by the Western Motor Coaches Limited, which is now plying for hire in and around the neighbourhood and making excursions to such places as Dunkery Hill Gate, Winsford, Cloutsham, The Doone Valley, Lynton, and other places (most unsuitable for such a coach). In doing so it has to traverse many narrow roads and lanes which at certain places it is impossible for any other vehicle to pass. The Coach is of considerable width heighth (sic) and length and bears a striking resemblance to a Hay Elevator ... [it is] likely to frighten horses and cause, as it has already done, accidents incurring thereby not only injury to property but also personal injuries to individuals.

The neighbourhood is well-supplied with horses and carriages for its requirements which enables a large number of residents to earn a livelihood and therefore such a coach is utterly unnecessary and totally unsuitable for this district. Your memorialists therefore humbly pray that your respective councils will prohibit the use of the existing coach and refuse to grant licenses to any other coaches of a similar character that may be applied for.

Among the signatories were many members of Minehead's gentry including the Baronne Le Clement de Taintegnies, Mr Blofeld who lived at Dunster Lodge and Mr T. Lovelace of Bratton Court. Tradesmen whose delivery vehicles might have been at risk included Isaac Floyd, draper; W.G. Batchelor, grocer and provision merchant and G.S. Balman, family butcher. Many hoteliers and inn-keepers who relied on visitors who came to the area for hunting, riding and driving signed the petition as well.

Among those who signed whose businesses were threatened by the ominous onslaught of the motor vehicle was William Preddy, saddler, whose premises were situated at 1 The Parade on the corner with Holloway Street. J.W. Ridler had taken over the Metropole hunting stables from Messrs Merson and Harding. All three signed. This was a business which relied on the hire of hunters, hacks and, of course, polo ponies.

Harold Langdon was the proprietor of perhaps the largest posting establishment in Minehead. His main premises were in Summerland Avenue. His two best known vehicles were the four-horse coaches,

Red Deer and Lorna Doone, which made regular daily runs between Lynton and Minehead. Bookings were taken at the GWR station and at Kinnersley's Fancy Stores in Wellington Square. The coaches left each day from the railway station as did Hobbs and Co.'s horse-drawn charabanc. Hobbs seems to have been part of the Langdon enterprise. The charabancs ran daily to Porlock Weir leaving at 11.55am and returning about 6.30pm. The fare was 2s 6d.

Mr Hobbs also hired out breaks, landaus and victorias and his advertisement in a contemporary guidebook states that both open or closed carriages could be sent to meet any train on receipt of a wire. All of these vehicles were apparently kept in the Summerland Road premises though I am not sure whether the horses were stabled there too. It isn't surprising that both Mr Langdon and Mr Hobbs signed the petition.

One person who didn't sign was W [?alter] Williams. Mr Williams had been a coach builder but round about the time of the petition it seems likely that he was turning his attention to the motor car. In a guidebook dated about 1911 he advertises himself not simply as a carriage builder but as a carriage and motor body builder and his premises are now known as Townsend Garage. A picture of a motor car appears alongside images of various carriages. Maybe he could see the way things were heading and didn't want to cut off his nose to spite his face.

Hardly a hay elevator but the shape of things to come!

114

I haven't yet found any evidence to tell me whether the petition was successful or not but although there were a few motor coaches running in the area before the 1920s it was the following decade that saw the real rise of the motor coach and the demise of Red Deer and Lorna Doone.

Revels and Wrestling

Sword and dagger at the Revels

Recently I was asked whether I could find out anything about Hawkridge Revel and, although I discovered only a little about that particular revel, I did unearth some information about revels in other parts of West Somerset.

Like church ales, revels date from the medieval period and a revel feast was still being held in nearly every village in West Somerset in the nineteenth century. These revels were originally held to celebrate the festival of the patron saint of the parish church. There are some notes about the date of Hawkridge Revel in the *Free Press* files, saying it was held on the Monday nearest the feast of the beheading of St. John the Baptist, 29 August, while Revel Sunday was on the Sunday which combined most closely with the feast of St Giles, 1 September. I would have expected the Revel Sunday to precede the Monday, but if we follow this ruling that wouldn't necessarily be so.

In fact, Hawkridge Revel was usually kept for up to three days and in 1946 an old inhabitant recalled that when the annual revel was held at Hawkridge there used to be gingerbread stalls in the village and 'folks went to service in church on the first day'. Wrestling took place during the revel and three farms sold beer. In 1960, an old board still hung over Mr Lock's workshop with the wording 'William Lock, Licensed to sell Beer and Tobacco' but the selling of beer was permitted only once a year when an occasional licence was granted to sell beer on Revel Sunday and the following day from the house adjoining the workshop. This was round about 1880.

When, in 1938, the revel at Hawkridge was revived with a gymkhana, clay pigeon shoot and skittling for a sheep in order to raise money for Hawkridge School, it was a pretty mild affair compared with the revels of the early nineteenth century. Then wrestling, cudgel fighting, bull baiting and cock fighting were the chief attractions together with more innocent pastimes like climbing the greasy pole, catching a sheep with a greasy tail and grimacing through collars.

At Wiveliscombe, the revels in the early nineteenth century seem to have been very carefully organised. In 1821, the revel was held on Trinity Tuesday and the list of subscribers, each paying between half a crown and five shillings, included such well known and respected names as Hancock, Boucher, Lutley and Culverwell. In 1826, posters advertised Ford Revel to be held 'on the close by the milestone' on Monday 17 July beginning at 2pm. The cash prizes raised by the subscribers were two guineas for both cudgel playing and wrestling and seven guineas for donkey racing. Seats were provided for the subscribers and carriages and horses were charged an admission fee. All proceeds from the event would be used for the benefit of the Public Infirmary and the Sunday School.

For the 1806 Wiveliscombe Revel, advertisements for wrestling and cudgel playing were placed in the *Sherborne Mercury* and wrestlers came to the town from all around: Exton, Huish Champflower, Skilgate, Winsford, Treborough, Bampton, Elworthy, Bishop's Hull. On this occasion, John Norman and James Sully of Exton shared the prize money with James Burrow of Landside.

Cudgel playing, or sword and dagger, was played with two sticks: in the right hand, an ash pole about three feet in length and the thickness of a man's forefinger, set into a basket hilt to protect the hand; and in the left, a stick, half the length and double the thickness, used primarily as a guard. The object of the game was to break your opponent's head and the moment the least drop of blood appeared on a player's face or head they were beaten and had to make way for the next challenger. At the same time, a great deal of damage could be done by experienced players simply beating the legs and lower bodies of less skilled youngsters.

Accounts for this 1806 revel show that a stage was set up and competitors provided with special shirts made for the occasion. The gloves, which were used from year to year, were padded with sheepskin. Anyone wanting to play would throw his hat into the ring and, according to a set of rules still in existence, had to be on the stage and quite ready to start within five minutes of throwing up his hat. The first two men to mount the stage were to play six bouts if 'no blood before'. The person on the stage was considered to have broken a head if no person came to play him within five minutes.

The 'person that shall fairly break the greatest number of heads and save his own' was to receive first prize while winning players entitled to shares in the prize could divide them or play them out as they agreed. The sticklers, presumably the referees, were to make the proper regulations and decide all disputes, if they were in agreement. If not, a majority of the subscribers present would make the decisions and were even entitled to 'make a new regulation during play' if need be.

Wrestling wild Exmoor style

At Lynton, round about 1850, the annual revel began on the first Sunday after Midsummer Day and wrestling was a chief feature in the amusements, as at most Exmoor revels. Large sums were raised by subscription to provide worthwhile cash prizes that would attract champion wrestlers from all over the area while in some parishes it was the custom for silver spoons to be bought as prizes.

In many places the wrestling bouts took place in the churchyard and notice of contests was often announced outside the church before service on Sunday mornings. Parson Jack Russell, rector of Swimbridge from 1832 to 1879 and who, as a young man, enjoyed wrestling, recalled arriving at a Cornish church one morning to take a service and seeing a man posted outside with six silver spoons stuck in a band in his hat, shouting: 'Plaize to tak' notiss. Thaise zix zilver spunes will be wrestled for next Thursday and all gan'lemen wrestlers will receive vair play.' Then he swaggered into church, went up in the singing gallery and hung his hat, with the spoons, on a peg where it was visible to the parson and whole congregation.

This was the practice at Countisbury in the 1830s where the silver spoons were hung in front of the gallery at Countisbury Church during divine service on Revel Sunday.

At Old Cleeve, in 1901, an old countryman recalled: 'When I was young, we would go out on the moor and have a turn just for the fun of the thing. You might get a broken arm or leg or get your eye put out with t'other chap's elbow but it was rare good sport. At the time of the revels you would see the champion come into church, with half-a-dozen spoons stuck in his hatband, prizes he had won in wrestling.'

'Yes,' chipped in another. 'And I've heard my father say that when the revels were on at Roadwater, he has seen a champion wrestler walk into Old Cleeve church and hang his hat, adorned with ribbons, on a nail in front of the gallery as a challenge to all-comers.'

At Knowstone and Exton wrestling of 'the most brutal order' took place for a beaver skin top hat which was displayed on the altar during afternoon service.

The wrestling seen on television these days is a milk-and-water affair compared with the barbaric wrestling of the last century which consisted of trying to kick your opponent while avoiding being kicked by him. The contestants would shake hands, toss a coin for the first kick and then stand with outstretched arms grasping each other's shoulders. They wore specially made heavy boots with wide toes and a strip of new leather, as hard as oak, sewn to the tips. A favourite trick in some places was to cut the upper of the boots away from the sole and insert a piece of tin with saw teeth before stitching the leathers together again.

At a given signal, the first kicker launched his blow on the enemy with all the force of a football player, and the second, if he had strength enough, kicked back in return and finally the two closed in for a fierce struggle to place the other on his back. It was in all respects a brutal fight save that fists were not used and old wrestlers were proud to show off their wounds which often consisted of crushed bones and huge scars which they carried to their graves.

Savage, writing in 1830, alludes to the revel at Exford where wrestling was the main activity and noted that the men 'do not pad their legs'. These revels were wild and there came a point round about the middle of the nineteenth century when 'many respectable inhabitants set themselves against the revels because of the brutality and drunkenness' and as a result they 'dwindled into insignificance.'

In some places, wrestlers colluded to share prizes and subscribers began to lose interest. Eventually, kicking was forbidden and at Captain Everett's annual wrestling match at Bridgetown in 1864 several hundred watched 12 wrestlers taking part in 'good old English style' rather than wild Exmoor style. By 1872, the revel at Oare was advertised as the 'usual annual diversions' including foot races, football and races in which 'fust in don't win' for ladies under 80.

Both Wootton Courtenay Revel and Culbone Revel had died out by about 1850. Until then, the latter was held in the churchyard with boxing, wrestling and sideshows and when Tom Cook talked to Bob Patten in about 1970, he reckoned it had been a 'fair booze-up'. Certainly the revels were considered to be no place for decent young women and some respectable farmers' wives forbade their girl apprentices to attend. 'There are no places so dangerous for girls.'

Second World War Secrets

Wartime secrets underground

As 1995 drew to its close, I looked back on a year during which celebrations to mark the 50th anniversary of the end of the Second World War took place in practically every community in West Somerset. Memorial services, exhibitions and wartime-style concerts and dances all sparked off many memories, not only of national events and personal heroism and grief but also of what it was like to be living here and 'doing one's bit' during the war years.

At Roadwater, the exhibition staged for VE day aroused so much interest and elicited so much information that it was felt that a permanent reminder of the events of the war was needed. As a result Clare Court, with enthusiastic help from many people, has produced a stylish book, *A Somerset Village in Wartime, Roadwater 1939-45*.

The book covers comprehensively all aspects of life in the village: the invasion committee, the evacuees, the knitting of 1700 garments (mostly for the Merchant Navy Comforts Fund), the dances at the village hall and, of course, the Home Guard. Originally the Local Defence Volunteers, or 'Look, Duck and Vanish' as they were often called, they were soon re-named and three Home Guard units were set up in the Roadwater area. I was particularly fascinated to read about the 'secret' Home Guard and to meet Mr Bob Reed, now of Watchet, who was a member of that unit until called up for active service early in 1942.

These 'secret' units were made up of men trained to use high explosives and there seem to have been several in West Somerset, perhaps because of its proximity to the Bristol Channel. Mr Reed was part of a small group sent to an army training centre at South Petherton for a weekend's training with explosives. He was issued with a revolver and live ammunition for use in an emergency and had to keep this a secret, even from his family, although his revolver was hidden in his bedroom at home.

More weekends were spent learning to use the revolver, to fire a Browning machine gun, to throw a hand grenade and to handle and detonate the ammunition used for blowing up railway lines and metal girders. The biggest problem was the sticky bomb. 'It was enclosed in a covering which was removed before throwing, with a handle that sometimes broke off when hitting the target. This made it useless. A time was allowed and then the person who threw the bomb had to blow it up!'

The ammunition was hidden underground. One of these hideaways was in the old slate quarry at Treborough and Bob Reed remembers the first time he was taken there. 'We ... entered the wood from the road on the east side to the left of the old lime kiln. We soon came to a high cliff, the base of which was banked up to ten to 12 feet. We crawled up the bank and got to a hole which reminded me of the entrance to a badger's sett.' Inside was a good-sized tunnel which had been cleared and cleaned out ready for use. Here was stored ammunition, sticky bombs and explosives and there was an emergency store of hard food rations. A little further in there were shelves which, if the worst came to the worst, could be used as bunks.

There was another hideaway at Lodge Rocks quarry but it is the one at Felon's Oak, Rodhuish, that catches my imagination. About a quarter of a mile above the crossroads, a metal bunker was set in underground in the high bank several yards from the lane. The entrance was through a trap-door on the top of the hut which was covered with earth. The army were responsible for installing these metal huts and it seems quite unbelievable that local people were not aware of what was going on, but they weren't. It was all hush-hush!

These were not the only secret hideaways in West Somerset during the war. Dr Francis Eeles, secretary of the Central Council for the Care of Churches and who lived in Dunster, was responsible for arranging secret and safe accommodation for many of the country's priceless treasures and archives. Twenty-nine lorry loads of furnishings and fittings from City of London churches, fonts, pulpits, screens and two complete organs, came to Somerset and most were stored in the vaulted cellars and vast out-buildings of St Audries School at West Quantoxhead. Another store was in the crypt of St Andrew's Church at Wiveliscombe, bone-dry and large enough for a lorry to be driven in. Lichfield Cathedral's eighth-century treasure, the precious Gospel Book of St Chad, was hidden there as well as wonderful stained glass from Exeter and Salisbury cathedrals and the fifteenth-century east window from St Peter Mancroft in Norwich. Archives, an entire library from the French Protestant Church in Soho Square, church plate and pictures were all concealed in the area while at Cleeve Abbey were stored 13 of the oldest bells in London, already survivors of the Great Fire.

6 CHRISTMAS CHEER

Mortals awake, rejoice and sing!

With all due deference to those people who band together and put in tremendous efforts to keep up the carol-singing tradition and give pleasure to listeners while collecting money for some really useful cause, I have to say that carol-singing is not what it used to be. And this lament is more than a century old.

Mr Marson, vicar of Hambridge, wrote in 1906 in a national newspaper: 'Carol-singing in Somerset has fallen into a flat and feeble rendering of the surprising songs of Moody and Sankey so that we are urged, even at midnight, to gather up sunbeams or to "Dare to be a Daniel". This to the great discontent of all the old crowders who relate hardy tales of their carol-singing days when they started in bands of 40 or 50, each with a pitcher, a-wassailing. They remember how they did bide up all night and dance, how when their pitcher had been filled with ale, cider, or cider-ginger-and-sugar, they would slip home to empty it and then come back to the wassailing.' Hambridge is, of course, near the heart of visiting wassailing country, Drayton, where the Somerset Wassail song was collected by Cecil Sharp in about 1905 and where wassailing, singing from door to door as opposed to apple tree wassailing, is still carried on.

Carol-singing was carried out according to parish tradition and practice. Usually the carollers were the village musicians; a band of singers and instrumentalists who led and accompanied the singing in church or chapel and accompanied dancing on high days and holidays. I was brought up in Warwickshire and experienced the tail end of the tradition there. The chapel carol party toured the village accompanied by a harmonium set on a handcart rather than the fiddle, clarinet and bass viol of earlier days and sang some of the old carols including Thomas Shoel of Montacute's 'Joy to the World' and my own favourite at the time, 'Rolling Downward through the Midnight'.

Lewis Court, writing in 1928 in *The Romance of a West Country Circuit*, describes how for Tom Slade, the Roadwater blacksmith, carol singing was the musical event of the year. The choir met to practise at his house and under his bidding 'sallied into the stillness of Christmas

Eve and woke the silences of the old farmsteads and halls with the glad strains of 'Behold! what glorious news is come!' or 'Mortals awake! rejoice and sing!' Tom insisted on perfect silence and stillness from the singers till the instruments struck up the great major chord right under the windows of the sleepers.

Even at the turn of the century, people were aware that the carolling tradition was fast disappearing and were collecting and recording the old carols just as they are today. Glyn Court's excellent *Westcountry Carols* includes carols from West Somerset as well as from further afield.

Some of the carols were familiar words set to different tunes. 'While Shepherds Watched by Night' is said to have been sung to nigh on 150 different tunes. Mr W. Dicker, the schoolmaster at Winsford at the turn of the century, noted in *Somerset and Dorset Notes and Queries* for 1904 that the tune 'Carolina', was a great favourite for 'While Shepherds' with the old singers of Dunster and the hill country of West Somerset. He copied it from a manuscript music book belonging to one of the old church singers at Dunster.

From the carolling tradition around Frome came these words, familiar, yet unfamiliar:

'What shall us sing? Sing all over One. What was One? One was God, the Righteous man. Save our souls! The rest Amen.'

What shall us sing? Sing all over Two: two was the Jewry, three was the Trinity, four Our Lady's bower, five the dead alive, six the crucifix, seven the lump of leaven, eight the crooked straight, nine water wine, ten golden pen, eleven gate of Heaven and twelve the ring of bells.

This song was considered a carol but 'The First Day of Christmas' was regarded more as a feat of memory. In a version recorded in the Blackdowns the partridge in a pear tree was replaced by 'a part of a juniper tree' while the growing pandemonium included eight hares a-running, nine bears a-biting and twelve bulls a-blaring.

Singing at Christmas was not all carol-singing. Often singers and musicians in the church and chapel galleries would try out a special new anthem for the day and woe betide them if, like Thomas Hardy's choir in Longpuddle church gallery, having been up all night, they fell asleep and forgot their cue. About 1745, John Broderip, organist and Master of Choristers at the cathedral church at Wells, published a new set of anthems and psalm tunes which he had composed for use in parish churches. Among local people who bought copies were the Revd Ryal and Henry and William Chilcott of Dulverton; the Revd Clare and Mr Franclyn of Minehead; Mr Murray, singing master of Stoyey [?Stowey] and the Revd Rogers of Withicombe. I wonder how many of their choirs performed Mr Broderip's 'A Hymn for Christmas Day' that year.

Christmas past

Two hundred years ago, in December 1799, the prospect of a merry Christmas must have seemed distant for many ordinary West Somerset folk. England had been at war with France for eight years, food generally was expensive and the price of bread astronomic.

It was bitterly cold over Christmas and at Over Stowey Parson Holland, writing in his diary, complained that it was 'so cold I cannot hold my pen.' On Christmas Eve it froze hard and the parson was furious with his servant, Robert, who went out to try to buy some butter which was very scarce and insisted on taking the great horse on the icy slippery roads. 'He will rot with laziness by and by,' commented the parson. He went on, 'The poor come for meat and corn this cold weather and against the Christmas Season. Some very thankful and others almost saucy. If a man had not some object beyond the gratitude of his fellow creatures he would never do a charitable act as long as he lived.'

On Christmas Eve the parson was 'much harried by the poor of the parish who come for Christmas gifts. Many persons rather in affluence come but this is not right because it takes from those who are real objects. The lower classes have no pride of this kind among them, and the Somersetshire lower classes less of this pride than any other.'

Christmas Day dawned cold, clear and frosty and at five in the morning the family at the vicarage was woken by carols sung by the church musicians. The parson celebrated the Sacrament at Over Stowey before riding over to Aisholt to take the service there in the afternoon. He returned to a solitary late dinner of sprats and a fine woodcock while in the kitchen poor neighbours and workmen enjoyed a good meal, staying until past ten o'clock and singing 'very melodiously'. He sent half-a-crown to his early morning serenaders.

A century later there was again little inclination to celebrate with abandon. The author of *Notes by the Way* wrote in the *Free Press* of 6 January 1900: 'England has seldom seen a sadder Christmas than that of the year just gone by. The air seems tremulous with the mournful cries of mothers bereaved; of wives and children who for ever, alas, must long in vain for the "touch of a vanished hand and the sound of a voice that is still". It makes our hearts run to water as we think of it. The remembrance of fallen heroes has been as the skeleton at the feast.' The Boer War had broken out a few months earlier and many Somerset men had gone to fight, my grandfather included.

Nonetheless there were the usual Christmas services and festivities and local gentry and clergy gave generously to the poor of the parishes. At Nettlecombe Sir W.J. Trevelyan and Mrs Trevelyan presented a representative of each family attending Yard school with a pair of boots. At Carhampton Mr Wilfred G. Marshall MFH presented to each family of cottagers a present of coals and to each of the elderly a present of money.

Up at Cutcombe the Christmas morning service was 'very bright' and fully choral with an anthem 'very tuneful and sung with expression and in good time'. The choir chanted the proper psalms – all of them – and the Athanasian Creed. They had been trained by the rector's wife, Mrs de Carteret, who had 'taken a great deal of trouble and put herself to much inconvenience' to have a bright service.

On the following Thursday a Christmas tree was provided for the children in the school room but the weather was wet and rough and many were unable to come. The tree was decorated with candles, tiny balloons and pretty ornaments and every child received a present, a cracker and an orange.

At Over Stowey in 1899 things were very different from a century earlier. One evening soon after Christmas the Stanleys at Quantock Lodge entertained about 80 people from the parish – choir, ringers, church workers, members of the Girls Friendly Society – to a substantial and abundant supper in the hall at the Lodge. After toasts and the singing of the National Anthem, all adjourned to the dining-room where a conjurer entertained. Watches, handkerchiefs etc. disappeared and reappeared in an astounding manner and a live rabbit popped out of an apparently empty hat. Dancing followed; every guest was given a present and the evening finished with carols. Was the Stanleys' eldest son with them to celebrate, I wonder, or had he already been killed in South Africa?

On the other side of the Quantocks at Nailsbourne an ancient tradition was coming to an end. There, for perhaps centuries, the cowman had sung his 'Mystery', the Beast Song, to the cattle in the barton on Christmas Eve. At Nailsbourne there was a Glastonbury Thorn that flowered on Old Christmas Eve to which, it was thought, all cattle and horses went, unless fastened, to kneel and worship; a belief held in many parts of the West Country.

By 1906 there was a new cowman who was considered unsuitable to receive the 'Mystery' and so it was passed to Ruth Tongue, later a collector of folklore.

Perhaps the new cowmen didn't believe the old legend. Which reminds me of the story of a man who'd come from another part of the country and who strenuously denied the possibility that the animals could be found on their knees in the barton on Christmas Eve.

'Why don't you go and look?' asked his companions.

'I shall,' he said.

On Christmas morning after church they asked him, 'Well, did you go?'

'Couldn't get there,' he replied. 'The lane was jammed up with cattle.'

Burning the ashen faggot

Until the beginning of the twentieth century, the burning of the ashen faggot at Christmas time was one of the most popular of Christmas customs. Everyone who records it – and many do – writes of the anticipation and excitement associated with the event.

Miss Alice King, the blind daughter of the rector of Cutcombe, writing not long before her death in 1894, described it as the most important West Country custom, 'indispensable on Christmas Eve in every properly constituted West Country farmhouse. No West Country farmer would have any good luck during the following year if the ashen faggot was not duly burnt at his house at Christmas.'

The burning of an ashen faggot rather than a yule log seems to be a custom peculiar to the West Country and, more particularly, to Somerset and Devon. There are several ideas about its origin. One is that it commemorates one or other of King Alfred's victories against the Danes and that afterwards the conquering army cut down branches of ash, the wood that will burn when green, to keep warm during the following night.

Another theory is that it was an ash fire that Joseph lit in the stable at Bethlehem to warm Mary and the baby Jesus and that the custom commemorates that event.

Obviously, the custom of burning the ashen faggot varied from village to village and family to family but there was a basic pattern.

First the ashen faggot itself. This was a fair-sized bundle of ash branches bound together with twisted ash whips. The size of the faggot would vary in length and diameter depending on the size of the fireplace for which it was destined but Alice King spoke of a 'goodly load of wood, such as might be a respectable burden for a Spanish mule crossing the Sierras.' When the faggot had been made up, it was sawn clean across at either end to make a neat bundle.

The ties, which as you will see were an essential part, not only of the faggot but of the custom, were occasionally made of hazel or even thorn, and the number varied. In Devon, the tradition seems to have been for there to be three – one at either end and one in the middle – but in parts of Somerset there was evidently no particular number and 'the more the better' seems to have been the rule in some inns where the custom was observed.

The day on which the faggot was burned also varied; generally Christmas Eve but sometimes Christmas Day and even New Year's Eve. Edward Fursdon, writing in *Country Life* in 1960, described the custom as he remembered it as a child:

'The faggot was burned after dinner on Christmas Eve and all gathered around the old fireplace wearing their best clothes and sitting in a half circle. The fire was spread out over the hearth to cover the length of the faggot. First, some old ash wood kept from the previous year was burned and, while this was happening, the youngest lad present picked up the new faggot and, starting with the eldest and continuing in strict order of age, handed it round. Each member of the family took it into his hands for a moment or two, choosing in his own mind which of the three binds would be the first to burst. Keeping this to himself, he then made a secret wish.

'When the round was complete and the old wood burned to embers, the new faggot was laid very carefully and squarely on to the glowing remains It was very important that the embers were spread out far enough at each end and raked to provide a consistent heat so that each band had the same chance. Then the family waited in anticipation for the moment when the first band would snap. The only sound was the hissing of the ash sticks as they began to swell in the heat. Eventually the first band went with a great crack and those who had chosen it would know that their wish would come true as long as they kept it secret. Soon the other bands would snap and the ash sticks would cascade out over the fireplace.'

In this particular family a handful of sticks was quickly seized from the fire, some to be saved until the next year. Then each member of the family took one and with a knife stripped off the bark. The year was written at one end and the owner's Christian name at the other and then the stick was added to his own personal bundle which contained a stick for each year of his life.

The children were then sent to bed and the rest of the party enjoyed an evening of merry-making: singing, dancing, telling tales and drinking 'cobler's punch', that peculiarly West Country mixture of cider and gin.

Ham, chicken, tongue etcetera pie

I've recently come across a typescript dated 17 November 1898, and headed 'The Old Fashion Devonshire Gammon Pie'. The writer was a Henry Parker of Watchet who, for some reason, seems to have been in Bridgwater when he wrote the account.

Henry Parker was probably born at Loosedon [Lewsdon?] Barton near Winkleigh in North Devon round about 1830 or maybe even before. He was certainly living there as a boy. W.G. Hoskins mentions that Loosedon was a Domesday manor and later a medieval mansion. Just what the house was like in the early 1800s I don't know.

Henry well remembered the labour and trouble his mother used to take in making one of these old fashion gammon pies every Christmas. It was a raised pie and it was huge. Ingredients included a large ham, the largest the farm could provide; three or four couple of chickens, jointed, and ox tongues etc. We can only guess at the etc, but presumably it referred not only to the seasonings and spices and forcemeat that were added but also to any other meat product that happened to be available; maybe a brace of pheasants or even a rabbit or two.

Henry's mother made a huge quantity of dough, for the bottom, sides and cover were all made of dough. It was demanding work and Mrs Beeton, in a recipe for a much smaller pie, states: 'To raise the crust for a pie with the hands is a very difficult task and can only be accomplished by skilled and experienced cooks.' Mrs Parker was clearly such a one. The pie was raised on a very wide plank or two planks fastened together and then the ham was placed in the centre with the pieces of chicken and tongue round about.

When the pie was ready and the huge oven sufficiently heated, it would take two powerful men to carry it. The oven would have been a baking oven of the kind common in many West Country houses, built into the chimney wall with its own flue leading to the main chimney. It was probably made of brick although the old oven could by then have been replaced by a purpose-built cloam (clay) Barnstaple oven, but I think this is unlikely since the Loosedon oven was clearly outsized.

The oven was heated, of course, by setting fire to a faggot of brushwood inside the oven and allowing it to burn to ash. By then the oven was very hot, the ash was scraped away and the bread put inside using a long-handled oven peel or, in this case, the pie was carefully inserted on its plank. Then the wooden, or maybe by this time iron, door would be closed and carefully sealed with clay and the pie left until done.

Once it was cooked, and we are not given any idea how long it might take, it would be placed on the long table in the hall. The pie was usually tapped by the Christmas waits on Christmas eve or morning, depending when they arrived. The waits consisted of the parish church choir augmented by others with good voices and some stringed instruments. Henry Parker remarks that the church choir had the reputation of being the best choir in North Devon at the time. They would go around to the farmhouses singing Christmas carols and did not usually arrive at Loosedon Barton until the early hours of Christmas morning. They sang a couple of carols under the windows and then one of them with a loud voice would wish the people a good evening or morning as the case might be. 'Mr and Mrs So-and-so we wish you a Merry Christmas and a Happy New Year, you and all your good family.'

The waits would then be called into the house to partake of the gammon pie. The pie was then kept on the table in the hall, and any and every person calling over Christmas (and callers were numerous) were invited to help themselves.

'I recollect too,' wrote Henry, recalling something which had clearly rankled for decades, 'that we boys (and there were several of us) used to get a poor share.' The pie was intended for 'visitors and callers and all were made most welcome and invited to eat, and drink as much nut brown ale and cider as they choosed. These were happy days, an old fashioned Christmas. Alas these are all passed away.'

And that was 1898!